About the Author

Louise McDonnell, an online and social media marketing expert, is passionate about delivering Facebook, SEO and website marketing training and coaching. She has a particular expertise in Facebook marketing having coached and trained over 2,000 businesses since 2009. In 2017, Louise was voted as one of the top worldwide 50 Facebook Marketing Bloggers by Feedspot.

Louise works with many Irish Government agencies including Failte Ireland, Enterprise Ireland and Local Enterprise Offices in Mayo, Sligo, Leitrim, Donegal and Roscommon. She also provides corporate training to businesses all over Ireland and online coaching to business owners all over the world.

Louise has over twenty years practical sales and marketing experience having worked with a wide range of businesses across multiple industry sectors. She speaks regularly at networking events and seminars on the subject of Facebook marketing.

This book, a culmination of Louise's expertise and experience, is guaranteed to help business owners become more proficient at Facebook marketing.

Louise lives in West Sligo with her husband and two children.

FACEBOOK MARKETING

The Essential Guide for Irish Organisations

LOUISE MCDONNELL

The Liffey Press

Published by
The Liffey Press Ltd
'Clareville'
307 Clontarf Road
Dublin D03 PO46, Ireland
www.theliffeypress.com

A catalogue record of this book is
available from the British Library.

ISBN 978-1-908308-99-3

Printed in Spain by GraphyCems.

CONTENTS

Contents

ACKNOWLEDGEMENTS

A big 'thank you' to the many people who supported me throughout the writing of this book. To all those who provided support, talked things over, read, wrote, offered comments, allowed me to quote them, shared their experiences and assisted in the editing, proofreading and design.

To all the businesses I have trained and mentored since 2009. Your need for practical guidance about Facebook marketing was the inspiration for this book. It took many years to fine-tune my approach. This book offers a step-by-step guide with useful advice that will help business owners, volunteers of community groups and digital marketing students.

Many thanks to David Givens for enabling me to publish this book. Thanks to Sarah, Brenda and David for helping me in the process of proofreading and editing, and to Alison for all the graphics and the book cover design.

Above all I want to thank my husband, Declan, and my children Jack and Ruth, who supported and encouraged me in spite of all the time it took me away from them. A special word of thanks to my mum, Brenda, who is always there when I need her. To my family and friends – thank you for listening to me talk incessantly about the book. It is finally a reality ...

Chapter 1

GETTING STARTED

1.0 INTRODUCTION

***Facebook helps you connect and share with
the people in your life.***

Facebook is astounding when you consider how it has impact-
ed and changed the way we communicate with each other.
Like it or not, you cannot deny that as a platform it offers businesses the opportunity to reach current and potential customers.

Facebook currently has 1.15 billion daily active users
worldwide. According to Facebook, there are 1.94 billion monthly
active users and 1.74 billion mobile monthly active users, and
66 per cent of Facebook users access their account at least once
a day. The average number of friends is 338. If you're in your
twenties you probably have over 600 friends. And the average
time spent per day is 20 minutes.

So all this presents an opportunity for businesses that want
to use Facebook to reach current and potential customers. The
problem is that Facebook is an incredibly busy and crowded
place. So the challenge for small businesses is figuring out how
they can stand out.

This book aims to tackle the issues that small business owners face when using Facebook as a marketing tool. Through my training and coaching work it has become clear that there is a high level of confusion amongst small business owners when it comes to using Facebook as a marketing tool. Many businesses have set up their Facebook accounts incorrectly and risk having them shut down by Facebook. Others run into security problems by sharing the same log-on details. Others don't know what to post or are totally lost when it comes to using Facebook ads. Many have completed Facebook training courses but haven't been able to apply the learning. And many businesses have a basic understanding of what they need to do but are overwhelmed and don't know where to start.

This book is for business owners and managers who want to become more effective at Facebook marketing. Whether they are complete beginners or have been using Facebook for a while with some success, business owners will be able to maximise the results they get from Facebook by following the advice provided in this book.

The book will help businesses by showing them how to:

- Become familiar with the architecture of Facebook
- Set up business pages and page administrators
- Understand the best use of page settings
- Carry out customer analysis and profiling
- Come up with compelling content that encourages potential customers to connect
- Raise brand awareness and generate sales
- Use Facebook ads effectively.

1.1 SHOULD YOU SET UP A BUSINESS PAGE?

Is Facebook for every business? No. It really depends on your customers. Do they use Facebook, and can you in turn use Facebook to get your brand in front of them?

If you manufacture spare parts for the automotive industry and your customers are a handful of car manufacturers around the world, then I would say Facebook is not an ideal marketing platform for your business. On the other hand, if your customers are likely to use Facebook regularly then you should consider integrating it into your marketing strategy.

Facebook works for both B2B (business to business) and B2C (business to consumer) customers. Some businesses will find marketing themselves easier on Facebook than others. It really depends on how open your customers are to 'hearing' about you and of course how good your efforts are. The key to having a successful Facebook business page centres around:

- Knowing who your customers are
- Understanding their needs and motivations
- Publishing content that resonates with them
- Building relationships with customers and potential customers.

Remember that customers will buy from you when they are ready to buy *not* when you are ready to sell. Just because you have a special offer does not mean that they have a requirement for your product or service at that moment. Rather than seeing Facebook as a place to push your products or services to potential customers, think of it as a place where you can remind customers that you exist so that when they *do* have a requirement for what you offer they will think of you.

1.2 REALISTIC EXPECTATIONS

Although there is no cost associated with setting up a Facebook page, Facebook is still not free. If you wish to have a successful Facebook business page you need to be prepared to allocate time every week to Facebook. You need adequate time to plan, prepare and publish content. Being successful on Facebook doesn't happen just by clicking your fingers.

Consider the time it takes to publish one really good post. Here are the basic steps:

- You need to consider the goal of the post. What do you want to achieve by publishing it?

- Next you need some time to be creative. How can you present this post in a way that it will stand out and appeal to your target audience?

- Then you need time to find an appropriate image or video, incorporate your logo and provide a call to action. What do you want your reader to do next?

- Next you need to come up with the copy (text) for your post. What are you going to say that will resonate with your audience?

- Then you need to consider the optimum time of the day to publish the post.

- Finally, you will need to review analytics to see how your post has performed.

The above could take from 40 minutes to an hour from start to finish. But remember: You can't expect to get results from your Facebook page if you don't schedule time in your diary every week.

Apart from publishing content, you will also need time to respond to comments and reply to messages.

It's also important to have a budget set aside for Facebook Ads, which will be covered later. Facebook Ads are a really powerful way of making sure that your business is reaching its target audience. Spent correctly, you can expect to get a really good return on investment from Facebook Ads.

1.3 COMMON ISSUES FOR SMALL BUSINESSES

Using a 'Personal Profile' Instead of a 'Business Page'

Some businesses mistakenly use 'personal profiles', in other words, they set up their business as an individual and send out friend requests to customers and potential customers. If you are set up like this you are in breach of Facebook's terms of use and your businesses profile could be removed. I know of numerous businesses and community groups that have had their pages removed because of this issue.

Then there are businesses that have a personal profile for their businesses but only use this profile to manage a business page. In this case they have both a 'personal profile' (friend page) and 'business page' for their business. They are not using the personal profile to promote their businesses so technically they should be okay? No is the answer here. There is a good chance that Facebook will remove the incorrectly set up personal profile and in this case the business will not have any way to administer its business page.

Sharing the Log-on Detail of the Owner's Personal Profile with Staff Members

Some business owners set up a personal profile for themselves and from there set up a business page. But then, they make the log-on details of their personal profile available to all staff members. So everyone in the business is using the one personal profile to update the business's Facebook page. There are a number of obvious reasons why this is not a good idea. First of all, if the business is using Facebook Ads they will have their debit or visa card associated with their account so anyone with the log-on details for this account will have access to these details. Secondly, if an employee leaves on bad terms it is leaving the organisation in a vulnerable position. Thirdly, it is limiting the exposure of your page. Employees can sometimes object to being made an administrator of a page because they don't want the business's customers to have access to their personal information. This simply will never happen. When an administrator publishes an update people who are not administrators of the page will never know who has published it. (Fig 1.1)

Fig 1.1

1.4 GETTING SET UP CORRECTLY

---

1. If you are new to Facebook, first set up a personal profile (friend page) for your personal use. Start using Facebook personally to gain an understanding of the terminology and architecture. Tune in to how your friends and family are interacting with each other and with other business pages.

2. Use your personal profile to set up business pages. You can have as many pages as you wish.

3. If your business already has a business page ensure that you are made an administrator. If you have been using a dummy profile to administer your page, make yourself an administrator of your page using your correctly set up personal profile and delete the dummy profile. Alternatively, if your dummy profile has lots of 'friends' you could consider changing the name of the profile to your own name.

4. Make any employees that will be working on your business page administrators of the page.

The ideal set up is that a business page has multiple administrators. Each administrator logs on to Facebook using their own log-on details. There is no limit on the number of pages that you can create or administer. Ideally, everyone has one set of log-on details to access their personal profiles and the pages they administer. These log-on details can be used on a desktop and on tablets/smart phones using the Facebook app, Pages Manager app, Facebook Groups app and Facebook Ads app.

In Chapters 2 and 3, I will explain how to get set up correctly and how to make staff members administrators of your page.

1.4.1 HOW TO CREATE A PERSONAL PROFILE

You can skip this chapter if you already have a Facebook 'Personal Profile'.

Navigate to www.facebook.com.

1. Register a Facebook Account (Fig. 1.2)

Under the words 'sign up' on the homepage, type your first name in the first box and your last name in the second box. Next enter a valid email address and re-enter that email in the box below. This will be used by Facebook to contact you to confirm your registration and for future communications. Next enter a password of your choice, your gender and your birthday. Then hit the Sign Up button at the bottom of the page.

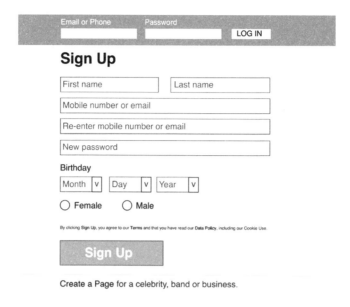

Fig 1.2

2. Confirm Your Email

A confirmation email will be sent to your email account. Open the confirmation email from Facebook, click on the link in the body of the email and it will take you to your new Facebook profile.

3. Find Friends

It's important to start making connections or 'friends' on Facebook right away. Remember, if you're a small business starting out on Facebook your friends will more than likely be the first people to like your business page.

You should limit your friends to people you know and trust. When you become friends with someone on Facebook you are giving them access to all your personal information like your email address, phone number (assuming you have these associated with your account), photos of your friends and family, and so on.

In order to become friends with someone on Facebook, one party must send the other party a 'friend request'. The person that receives the 'friend request' can confirm, delete or ignore the request.

If you're worried about your privacy on Facebook, you can set your account to only be 'visible' to your Facebook friends.

One of the first processes Facebook uses to find people that you know on Facebook is to search through your email address book. It will match email addresses of your contacts to people who also have Facebook profiles. You will then have the option of sending then a 'friend request'. (Fig. 1.3)

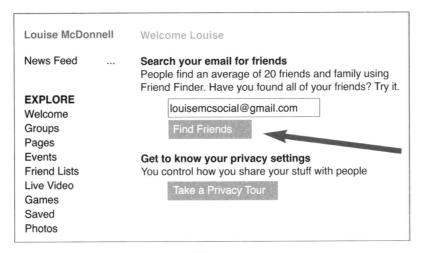

Fig 1.3

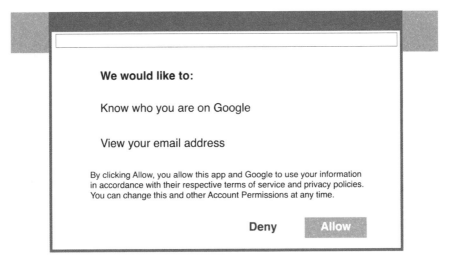

Fig 1.4

In step 2 Facebook will ask you to fill out your profile info. This includes your high school, home town, city you currently live in, the third level institution you attended and your employer. Facebook will use the information you make available in this section to find people you know. People who attended the same school at the same time as you, people living in the same city/town, people who went to college with you. Facebook will present a list of people you potentially know and you will have the option to send them a friend request.

In the update info/about section you will be asked for more information in relation to

- Work and education
- Places you've lived
- Contact and basic info
- Family and relationships
- Details about you
- Life events.

Facebook will use this information to link you up with people you know. You can choose to leave these fields blank if you wish.

1.4.2 How to Set Up a Profile Image

Add a profile picture. Click on the picture tab to upload a picture from your computer, tablet or smart phone. Cover images and profile pictures are both public and anyone visiting your page will be able to see them.

1.4.3 How to Set Up a Cover Image

Add a cover picture. A cover is the large image at the top of your profile. Click 'add a cover' and then choose whether you want to upload a new photo or pick one from one of your existing photo albums. Once you choose a photo, you can reposition it by clicking on the image and dragging it up or down and then click save.

1.5 SETTING UP A FACEBOOK BUSINESS PAGE

1. Login to your personal Facebook account.

2. On the upper right corner of your page click the downward facing arrow .

3. Select 'create page'. (Fig. 1.5)

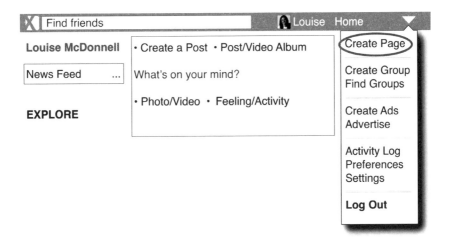

Fig 1.5

4. Choose a business category that is most relevant to your business. There are six options:

    *   Local Business or Place
    *   Company, Organisation or Institution
    *   Brand or Product
    *   Artist, Band or Public Figure
    *   Entertainment
    *   Cause or Community.

5. Insert your Facebook web address (this will appear after the facebook.com URL so it will look something like this: www.facebook.com/yourbusinessname).

6. Add a profile picture. Next you'll be asked to upload a picture. This will serve as the main visual icon of your page, appearing in search results and alongside any comments you publish. While any perfectly square image will work, the recommended size is 170 x 170 pixels, though I recommend uploading at least double that size for better quality. If you are a sole trader consider using a professional photo for your profile picture. Brands and bigger companies should use their logo. If your logo is rectangular in shape I recommend getting a square or stacked version created for use across all your social media platforms.

7. Add to Favourites (optional). Every individual Facebook user has a vertical navigation bar to the left of their news feed. You can add your business page as a 'favourite' item here – similar to bookmarking a web page in your web browser – for easy access.

8. Reach more people. Facebook will prompt you to create an advertisement to draw attention to your page. Whether employing paid tactics is part of your strategy or not, it's best not to add any ads at this stage. There's no compelling content on the page yet that would convince customers to ultimately 'like' your page. We will come to Facebook Ads in Chapter 5.

9. Add a cover picture. Use a cover picture that represents your brand and communicates your value proposition. According to Facebook, the recommended file is a JPG file that's 851 pixels wide, 315 pixels tall and less than 100 kilobytes. It's also recommended that there is:

- No contact information
- No 'calls to action' (book now, call here to order)
- No arrows pointing to the like button.

The cover image should reflect your business and be a strong representation of your brand. It can be seasonal or you can use it to promote upcoming events or milestones in your business.

Facebook recently introduced cover videos for business pages. The recommended size of a video is now 820 x 462 pixels, however it must be at least 820 x 312 pixels. According to Facebook, it introduced cover videos to create more engaging interaction and drive a richer experience for audiences. Cover videos enable businesses to shine a spotlight on one of the most prominent positions on their pages.

1.6 GIVING OTHERS ADMINISTRATIVE ACCESS TO YOUR PAGE

There are five different types of roles for people who manage Facebook business pages: Admin, Editor, Moderator, Advertiser, Analyst, Live Contributor. The Admin role has the highest level of control. Page admins can:

- Add and remove page admins
- Edit the page
- Add and remove apps to the page
- Create and delete posts as the page
- Go live as the page from a mobile device
- Send messages as the page
- Respond to and delete comments and posts to the page
- Remove and ban people from the page

- Create ads
- View insights
- See which admins have published posts on the page.

For a breakdown on the different roles see the table below. For more on page roles see section 1.7.

	Admin.	Ed.	Mod.	Adv.	Anal.	Live Cont.
Add and remove page admins	✓	✓	✓	✓	✓	
Edit the page	✓	✓				
Add and remove apps to the page	✓	✓				
Create and delete posts as the page	✓	✓				
Can go live as the page from a mobile device	✓	✓				✓
Send messages as the page	✓	✓	✓			
Respond to and delete comments and posts to the page	✓	✓	✓			
Remove and ban people from the page	✓	✓	✓			
Create ads	✓	✓	✓	✓		
View insights	✓	✓	✓	✓		
See which admins have published posts on the page	✓	✓	✓	✓	✓	

Rather than giving staff members the log-on details to your personal profile it is advised to make them administrators of your page. Choose from the five different options above depending on the level of control you wish to allow.

You can remove administrators any time when circumstances require it.

1.6.1 How to Make Your Staff Administrators of Your Page

To make someone an administrator (Admin, Editor, Moderator, Advertiser or Analyst) navigate to the settings panel of your page (see Fig. 1.6).

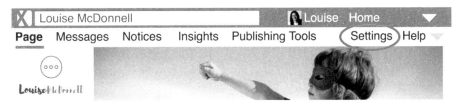

Fig 1.6

On the left hand side menu select the option 'page roles'. (Fig. 1.7)

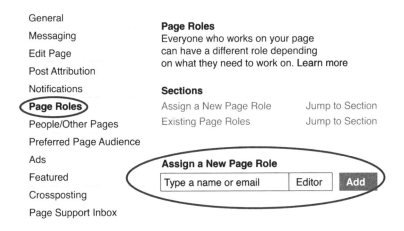

Fig 1.7

Before you can make anyone an administrator they must 'like' your page and have a Facebook personal profile themselves.

Type the name or email address of the person you wish to give administrative access to. If you are not 'Facebook friends' with the new administrator you will need to use the email address they use for Facebook.

The default role is set at 'editor'. Click on the dropdown menu to the top right of 'editor' to select the level of control you wish to allow.

1.6.2 Staff Concerns About Being Made an Administrator of Your Page '

Sometimes staff members are concerned about having their personal profiles associated with their place of work. Everyone's Facebook accounts (profiles) contain personal, sometimes sensitive information like age, date of birth, address, marital status, connections with others, groups affiliations as well as photos of loved ones. But none of this becomes available to employers, other Facebook page administrators or fans of any page you administer.

Being an administrator of a page means staff can create posts on the page and, depending on the level of administrative access, they can edit settings, respond to comments and messages and update the 'about' section of the page. When posts are published on the page the name of the person who has published each post is only available to other page administrators. The general public (anyone not an administrator) cannot see who has published the posts on the page. (Fig. 1.8)

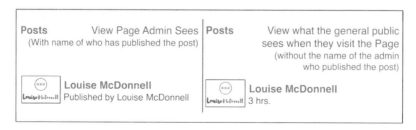

Fig 1.8

When set up correctly staff members only require one set of log-on details. This makes it much easier to post updates to a page using smart phones via the Facebook app or Pages Manager app.

1.7 PAGE SETTINGS

You will find the settings section at the top right hand side of your page (see Fig. 1.6).

Shortcuts/Favourites

When you pin your page in this section it will appear as a shortcut on the left hand navigation panel under your personal profile.

Page Visibility

You can unpublish your page by turning off its visibility.

Visitor Posts

This is where you control who can publish to your page. You can turn on or off the ability of visitors to publish. If you're worried about possible negative comments then perhaps this is an option. In general, though, it's good to encourage visitors to engage with your page. Facebook is a social network. It's a place where we should be having conversations. There is also an option to review posts by other people before they are published to the page. It is worth noting that when someone publishes a post to your page, it doesn't go into the news feed. The only way this will happen is if you 'share' the post. Otherwise it will sit in an 'others' news feed and more than likely will only be seen by you or anyone who looks at the 'others' section of your page (see Fig. 1.12).

Audience Optimisation for Posts

This is a feature that lets you determine the most relevant audience for your posts. According to Facebook it does not restrict the organic reach. The key to success on any page is to achieve high engagement levels on every post. This tool will help you achieve this as you can show the post to any audiences you believe might be interested.

So if you have a hair salon and you're posting about a new hair product that you assume will only be of interest to females under 25, you can select this audience. People you presume will not have any interest won't see this post so the engagement performance levels for this segment of your audience will not be affected.

If you have over 5,000 likes on your page this feature is automatically turned on. For pages under 5,000 likes you can turn this feature on in your settings.

When you are posting select the 'preferred audience' option which is to the right of the location icon as can be seen below. (Fig. 1.9)

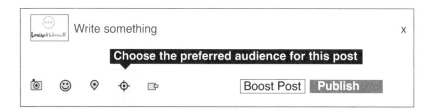

Fig 1.9

You can then choose people you would like to reach in the news feed based on 'interests'. There is a second tab which enables you to set restrictions based on age, gender, location and language. (Fig. 1.10)

Preferred Audience **Audience Restrictions**

Limit who can see this post. Only people in the audiences you choose can see this post anywhere.

Age

| 13 | 65+ |

Gender

All | Men | Women

Locations

| Include | Add locations |

Languages

| Enter a language |

Fig 1.10

Messages

You can turn on or off the ability of people to leave messages on your page. For most businesses this is a useful feature as it enables customers and potential customers to make enquiries. You will find that the more active your page, the more likely you are to receive enquiries.

Under the 'messaging' setting, which is found under the general settings, there are further options to configure the messaging function of your page.

If visitors to your page see a quick response rate they are more likely to send messages to your page. You need to respond to at least 75 per cent of the messages within a day or less in order for Facebook to show a response time on your page.

Facebook offers the option of setting up automatic responses which will make your page appear more responsive. The first option enables you to send an automated message when your office is closed or when you're away from your computer/phone. The second option gives an instant reply to any messages on your page. You can use this feature to let people know you'll respond within a certain time frame and therefore manage their expectations. The third option enables you to show a message greeting which is what people will see the first time they open a conversation with you on messenger.

You have up to 250 characters to customise all automated responses on your page.

Tagging Ability

This setting allows you to turn on or off the ability of visitors to your page to 'tag' their friends in photos and videos. When people tag their friends in this way it appears in their news feed and is an effective method for increasing the reach of your posts (the number of people who see them). Tagging is a great way of having conversations on social media. It's also a useful way of monitoring what other pages are saying about you.

Page Location for Frames

You can select if you wish to allow other people to use your page as a location for frames.

Country Restrictions

Use this setting to specify countries for which you wish your page to be restricted.

Age Restrictions

If you wish to set an age restriction or if your product is alcohol-related you can specify this here.

Page Moderation

You can block posts or comments to your page that contain specific works. You can list the words in this section.

Profanity Filter

Block the use of bad language on your page by turning on the profanity filter. Depending on your organisation, you can turn this feature off, set it to medium or high.

Similar Page Suggestions

When this feature is turned on Facebook will show your page as a suggestion to people who have liked similar pages. Likewise, when someone likes your page Facebook will suggest others to them.

Page Updates

Turn this feature off if you don't wish posts to be published on your page when you update page buttons, description and contact information.

Posts in Multiple Languages

Should you wish to allow people who manage this page to publish posts in multiple languages you can set this up here.

Comment Ranking

You can choose whether you wish comments on posts to be shown in chronological order or based on engagement levels, with more importance being given to verified pages and profiles.

Content Distribution

This feature enables you to prohibit people from downloading videos that you have saved to your page. Note though that it is only possible to download videos from pages in certain countries and not at all possible using a smart phone.

Download Page

It's possible to download pages posts, videos, images and page info. Usually this feature is used by people who are about to remove their page or merge it with another.

When you download your information, Facebook requires you to confirm your identity before you can complete the process. Facebook will send an email to the address that's listed on your Facebook account to ensure that you initiated the process. Once you receive the email, you will have to re-enter your password.

Merge Pages

You can merge duplicate pages so long as they represent the same thing. In order to merge pages:

- You need to be an administrator of both pages.
- The page names need to be as similar as possible.
- Both page addresses must be the same if your business has a physical location.
- Although Facebook does not specify it, I recommend that both pages have the same short and long descriptions. The more similar the pages look the more likely Facebook will approve the merge.

When your pages merge the people who like your pages and any check-ins will be combined, but posts, photos, reviews, ratings and the username will be deleted from the page you merge. The page that remains will be the same except for the addition of 'page likes' and 'check ins' from the page you have merged. Once a page is merged it's not possible to undo the merge.

Remove Page

Deleting your page means that it will be removed from Facebook and it will not be visible to anyone. If you choose to remove a page you'll have 14 days to restore it if you choose. After 14 days Facebook will ask you to confirm if you want to delete the page permanently. If you're unsure whether you want to remove the page or not another option is to unpublish the page whereby it will only be visible to admins of that page.

Messaging Settings

In this section you can set up how people can message your page. Set up the 'response assistant' to send instant replies to customers. This can be a great way of setting expectations for customers by letting them know when you are likely to respond to private messages.

Messages can be personalised by adding a person's name as well as your website address, phone number and address.

Select the 'change' button to personalise your instant response. (Fig. 1.11)

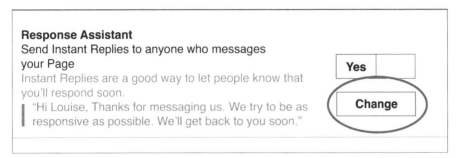

Fig 1.11

Edit Page

In this section you can set up a template for your page. There are templates for shopping pages, business pages, venues, politicians, services, restaurants and cafes. Each template has different tabs and buttons on the toolbar. For example, the shopping template has a 'shop tab' where businesses can feature products to sell on Facebook or by linking them to an ecommerce store.

Facebook is likely to develop this multi-tab approach to Facebook business pages. A business page is becoming more like a website with multiple pages to showcase products, services, events, etc. Google is also beginning to index each of these tabs as individual web pages.

Once a template has been selected for your page, you can choose to use the default tabs for that template or customise the look of your page by turning tabs on or off. Tabs can be reordered by moving their position in this section.

Post Attribution

The default setting is that posts, comments and likes on your page will be attributed to the page. Visitors to your page will not see who (which administrator) has posted updates on your page. You can change this to set the default to be your personal profile so that all posts, comments and likes on your page come from you personally. If you post to your page as yourself it will not go into the page's news feed but instead into the 'visitors' posts' section of your page. (Fig 1.12)

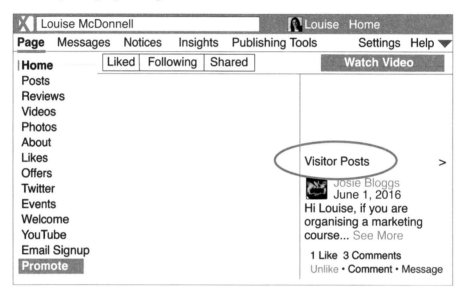

Fig 1.12

It is possible to switch attribution between your page and personal profile by selecting the attribution option on your page (Fig 1.13). In settings you can simply set the default which works best for you.

Top tip: If the default is set to your personal profile it can cause issues using your mobile phone to update your page.

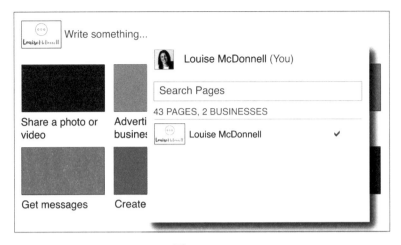

Fig 1.13

Notifications

It is possible to manage what notifications you prefer to receive from Facebook for your page. You can select how often you want to receive notifications regarding page activty. There are three settings: each time there is activity on your page, every 12 to 24 hours, or you can set it to off.

You can also select what you want to be notified about. Options include:

- New checkin from users
- New mention of page
- New reviews
- New comments on page post
- Edits to comments you have written
- New subscribers to events
- New followers of page
- New likes on page post
- New likes
- Edits to posts you have written
- New shares on page posts.

Message Notifications

You can turn notifications on or off for messages. If you turn on notifications for messages you will never miss a message and by responding quickly can maintain a high response rate on your page. Visitors to your page are more likely to send private messages if the response rate on the page is high.

Page Roles

Make other people administrators of your page in this section. There are five levels of access that you can select from depending on how much control you wish to allow (see section 1.6).

To assign a new page role:

- The person you are making an admin (Admin, Editor, Moderator, Advertiser, Analyst, Live Contributor) must first 'like' the page.

- If you are friends with them, you can simply type their name into the 'assign a new page role' dialogue box.

- If you are not friends with them, type in the email address they use to log into their Facebook personal profile into the dialogue box.

- Once you have inserted the person's name or email address into the dialogue box, select the level of admin access you wish to confer.

- You will be asked to type in your password to confirm this. This is a security measure.

- The new page admin will receive a notification on Facebook or an email to the account that is linked to their Facebook profile. They will need to accept the new role.

- As a security measure, new page administrators are restricted from making some administrative changes on the page, like adding or removing new admins for two weeks.

People and Other Pages

In this section you can see the people and pages that like your page. You can also see the date they liked your page, remove them from your page likes, ban them from your page or make them a page admin. There is also a search bar.

Preferred Page Audience

You can set the preferred audience you wish to reach on Facebook. This will not impact on the organic reach of your page but will assist Facebook to get your page in front of people you believe will be most interested.

You can specify which country, age group, gender, language and interests to create a preferred audience. There are thousands of options enabling you to target people based on their interests, activities, the pages they have liked and closely related topics.

Apps

It's possible to add third part apps to your Facebook page. These apps appear as tabs on the left side of your page. Depending on the app's settings, you may be able to edit the tab's name and image.

Some apps are free with paid for versions with additional functionality. If you decide to install an app on your page, check regularly that it is working. Facebook changes its architecture frequently, so it's best to check all apps after every new update. I regularly encounter pages that have installed apps over the years and now they no longer work. This looks unprofessional.

Instagram Ads

Instagram, one of the leading online mobile photo sharing, video sharing, and social networks in the world is owned by Facebook. One of the options available to you when you are placing ads on Facebook is to display them on Instagram. Under this setting you can link your ads with your Instagram account. This will help you to connect with other people on Instagram and grow your following with your target audience.

Featured

Up to five pages that you have liked as your page are displayed. You can select which pages you wish to display on your page and in what order. If you're a hotel and have one general page for the hotel and a separate page for your leisure centre, it's a useful feature for cross promotion between your two pages. It's also useful if you have more than one business or if you want to display pages relating to suppliers, stakeholders or businesses nearby.

Crossposting

This is a useful feature if you want to share videos across multiple pages. Pages need to 'add' each other before crossposting of videos is enabled.

1.8 ABOUT SECTION OF YOUR PAGE

---

1. Get the Right Categories

Choose a category that best matches your business. It will have an impact on how your page performs for searches on Facebook. You have to choose from a list of predefined categories. Choose up to three categories that best match your business.

2. Make Your Name Clear

This is the name of your page (not to be confused with your username). I recommend using your business name. Avoid including words like 'official' or any sales jargon as this may make it difficult for people to find your page.

3. Claim Your Username

When you claim a username it makes it easier for people to find your page as usernames, unlike page names, are unique. Your username combines with the Facebook web address to create a unique vanity URL for your page. If you haven't claimed your username the URL for your page is probably something like www.facebook.com/yourbusinessname-12345678910. If you have claimed it the vanity URL for your page is www.facebook.com/username. So for example my username is LouiseMcDSocial so therefore my vanity URL is www.Facebook.com/LouiseMcDSocial.

Vanity URLs are indexed by search engines like Google, so claiming your username will assist the search engine optimisation (SEO) of your page. If you are a small business without a website having a Facebook page that performs well for your business name is important in terms of your visibility on the web for searches relating to your business name.

Once you have claimed your username you can use it to direct people to your page. Use it on email signatures, business cards, posters, brochures, flyers, etc. It's particularly useful if you need to give a sound byte to the media. I recommend using your vanity URL everytime over the 'find us on Facebook' icons.

Try to keep your username close to your business name or business website address. Not only will this help people find you it will also make it easier for people to tag you on Facebook. When someone tags your business page in their comments it creates a link to your page. If your username is unlike your business name, it will limit the number of tags for your page.

Usernames are unique so if your business name has already been claimed you will need to come up with a variation. You might add in your town or country after your business name. Always add in an additional word after your business name rather than before as this will facilitate searches and tagging by others on Facebook.

Tip: choose your username wisely as Facebook limits the number of times it can be changed.

4. Enter Your Start Date

Let visitors to your page know when your business was founded (or you can choose from born, started, opened, created, launched, etc.). This is useful if you want to let visitors to your page know how long you've been in business or if you have some history associated with your business. It can be a great way of differentiating yourself from your competitors.

5. Fill Out the Hours of Operation

Fill out your hours of operation here. Remember, if your hours change throughout the year to keep this section updated. The last thing you want is disappointed customers turning up to your business, having consulted the opening hours on your Facebook page, when you're closed.

6. Pack the Short Description Full of Your Products and Services

Use this field to list your products and services. Avoid repeating your business name or address as these details are listed in other fields on your page setup. At one point Google used the first 8 to 10 words of this field in search results relating to your page.

7. Communicate Your Value Proposition in Your Long Description/Company Overview

It's important to use this field to communicate why potential customers should use you. What's unique about your business? What do you do better than others? Imagine your ideal customer was reading your long description. What could you say to them that would convince them to choose to do business with you?

Included keyword phrases in this field can increase the visibly of your page for related searches.

8. Use the Services Tab to Highlight Your Offering

This section enables professional services businesses to highlight a list of their offerings at the top of their page. It showcases to visitors to your page what you can do for them.

9. Think about the Call to Action Button

Ideally, what action do you want visitors to take when they visit your page? The 'call to action' is a prominent button found at the top of your page. It encourages people to take action and has been designed for mobile use as well. You can choose customers to:

- Book now
- Call now
- Contact us
- Send message
- Use app
- Play game
- Shop now
- Sign up
- Watch video
- Send email
- Learn more.

1.8.1 REVIEWS

Reviews are great. They let visitors to your page know what other people think about your business. People tend to give more credence to what others say about you rather than what you say about yourself.

Having lots of positive five star reviews on your page looks good to outsiders. It can give confidence to potential customers and be a useful tool to get prospects 'over the line'. Encourage good reviews by asking 'delighted' customers to post a review to your page. If people are into Facebook and posting reviews, chances are they will. Set a policy in your company that any time a customer gives positive feedback to you or your staff that they are encouraged to post a review on your page.

On the flip side, if you have a number of negative reviews on your page, you need to question why. Is there an issue you need to address in your organisation? What is at the root of these negative reviews? Were customers' expectations unrealistic? Is there an issue with a staff member? Is there an issue with your product/service quality? Can the issues raised be addressed by providing staff training, reviewing internal processes, changing product suppliers, etc.?

Visitors to your page will generally discount one negative review if all others are positive. However if there are many negative reviews then this is something you should not ignore.

Never respond to a negative review when you're annoyed or upset. Wait until you have calmed down and can respond to the review in a more objective frame of mind! Remember that your response will be visible to visitors to your page and people are often interested in how you respond to negative feedback.

You may want to thank the reviewer for their feedback and acknowledge the issue they had. Explain the processes you have put in place to ensure the problem (if your organisation is at fault on this occasion) doesn't arise again. In general, it is best not to offer any compensation as this can encourage more negative reviews.

1.9 MANAGING A FACEBOOK PAGE USING A SMART PHONE

Many small business owners use their smart phone to manage their Facebook page on the go. In fact, some small business owners only use their smart phone or tablet to update their page.

There are a number of apps available to make managing your page easy from your phone.

Pages Manager

Available for iOS and android, you can create and manage Facebook pages using your smart phone. Use this app to:

- Manage multiple pages easily using the one set of log-on details
- Update your page
- Schedule posts
- Respond to comments and reviews
- Upload photos, screenshots or videos from your phone
- View insights
- Respond to messages
- Boost posts.

Ads Manager App

This app allows you to manage your Facebook ads on the go. You can use this app to:

- Track ad performance
- Edit existing ads
- Edit ad budgets and schedules
- Receive push notifications
- Create ads.

Benefits of Managing Your Page from Your Phone

I remember meeting a business owner who told me that he used to take photos for his Facebook page using his phone. Then he would download the images to his laptop and upload them to his page from there. I made his life much less complicated when I introduced him to the Facebook Pages Manager.

- What I really like about the Pages Manager is that, unlike the Facebook app, you can only post as your page on your page. So when I want to update my page it comes from my page rather than my personal profile. When you post as yourself on your page it does not go into the news feed but instead sits under the 'visitors posts' section. Using the Pages Manager eliminates the chances of this happening.

- Pages Manager enables you to create posts quickly which is important for small business owners who are responsible for every aspect of running their business, not just marketing.

- If you and your staff are set up as page administrators/editors, when they download Pages Manager and log in they will be able to start updating your page straight away.

- Pages Manager is very useful for uploading images and videos and for using Facebook Live.

- Hair salons can use it to showcase 'before' and 'after' images of clients. Simply take a photo of your client, without displaying their face, and upload. Clothes shops can quickly take photos of new stock as it arrives. Businesses in the tourism sector can upload interesting landscapes of their area throughout the seasons. This will help keep your brand top of mind with your target audience. Business professionals can record a video of 'top tips' and publish it on their page. All Facebook page owners can also broadcast 'live' on their pages using the Facebook Live function on their phones.

1.10 UNDERSTANDING THE FACEBOOK NEWS FEED AND ALGORITHM

Facebook is a busy place. Most users have a few hundred 'friends', 'like' many pages and are members of a number of groups.

Your news feed is made up of:

- Updates from your 'friends'
- Updates from pages you have liked
- Updates from groups you have joined
- Posts that your friends have shared
- Facebook Ad posts.

A complex algorithm called 'Edgerank' controls what you see on Facebook. Facebook is such a busy platform that without this algorithm your user experience wouldn't be so positive. Imagine that this algorithm is acting like a newspaper editor. The editor's role is to sift through all the news items and make a call on what will be published. Only the most newsworthy stories get published. Edgerank is doing the same on Facebook. Every Facebook user's news feed is individual to them. Facebook knows what you are interested in based on your activity; what you 'like', 'comment on', 'share' and 'click'. If you regularly interact with a page because you find their content interesting, you will find that their posts tend to appear in your news feed. On the other hand, if you have liked pages in the past and have not interacted with their posts you will see their posts less frequently and perhaps not at all.

Your challenge as managers of Facebook pages is to produce content that your audience (the people who like your page) engages with. You need your audience to 'like', 'comment on', 'share' or 'click' on your posts to ensure they continue to see them.

1.10.1 Who Sees Your Posts and Why?

Once you set up a page your first challenge is to get people to 'like' or 'follow' your page. People who 'like' your page automatically become 'followers'. This means they are counted as a page 'like' and may see the posts published on your page in their news feed. People can choose to 'follow' your page but not 'like' it. In this scenario they may see your page posts but are not counted as a page 'like'. Fans of your page can unfollow your page but remain as a page 'like'. This means they are counted as a page like but will not see your content very often.

So if you have a page with 100 followers, when you post on your page you have the potential to reach this audience. If you have 1,000 followers you have the potential to reach 10 times more people. If any of your page likes should share your post you have potential to reach beyond your page likes audience, as your post will appear in the news feed of anyone who has shared your post, therefore reaching their friends.

But just because someone has 'followed' your page does not mean they are guaranteed to see your posts. They will only see your posts if Facebook believes they are interested in your content. Facebook's algorithm, Edgerank, decides whether or not your posts are seen in the news feeds of your page followers.

Although Facebook is constantly tweaking Edgerank, there are some basic factors which determine whether or not your fans see your posts:

- How often your fans interact with the posts you publish on your page.

- How popular a post is in general. If you publish a post and your fans start engaging with it immediately (liking, commenting, sharing, viewing or clicking), Facebook knows the content is good and is more likely to show it to more people. In this case fans who haven't seen your posts in a while may be reached. Posts that achieve high engagement levels quickly tend to stay longer in the news feed.

- The algorithm prioritises posts of friends and family in the news feed.

- Facebook has been prioritising instant articles and video posts in the algorithm over posts with external links, which take the user outside of Facebook's walls.

1.11 FACEBOOK GROUPS

Facebook offers the facility to set up 'groups' to facilitate communication between people who have a shared interest in a particular topic, organisation or cause. You can create a group ...

- For a party or family event
- To update and facilitate feedback from members of your staff
- For committee members to share information
- For a book club
- To update your customers
- To buy and sell items
- For schools.

1.11.1 HOW TO SET UP A GROUP

1. Go to the drop down menu at the top right of your profile. Select 'create group'. (Fig. 1.14)

2. Next you will be prompted to name your group, add some people and select the privacy (public, closed, secret). (Fig. 1.15)

3. The next step is to choose an icon to represent the group. This step can be skipped if you cannot find an appropriate icon.

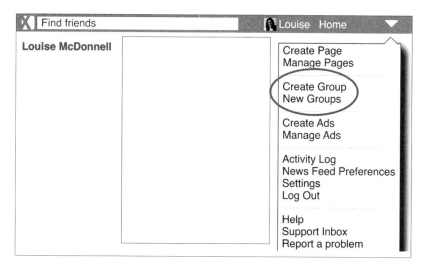

Fig 1.14

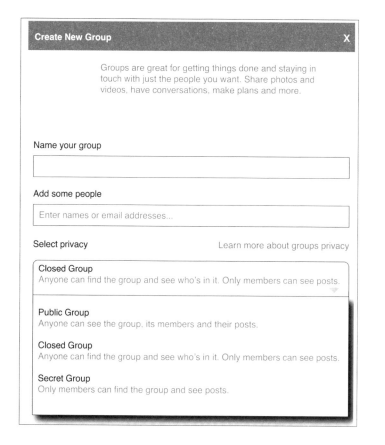

Fig 1.15

4. Personalise your group by adding a cover image. Currently the cover image must be at least 1,602 pixels wide by 500 pixels tall. (Fig 1.16)

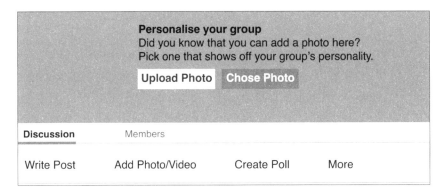

Fig 1.16

5. Add a group description to inform members what the group is about. Use this to communicate the group's objectives and to set parameters for what members can and can't post. This is important if you want members to provide peer support for each other but eliminates people using the group to spam group members.

6. Up to five tags can be associated with the group. This assists Facebook to index the group (with the exception of secret groups) for relevant searches and also lets group members know what the group is about. (Fig 1.17)

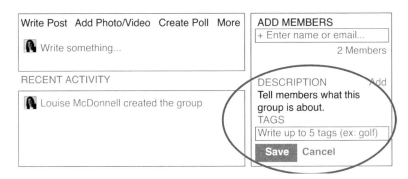

Fig 1.17

7. Adding and deleting members. There is an 'add members' section just below the cover image on the right hand side of the group page. You can add people who are your Facebook friends or by using their email address. For all types of groups (public, closed and secret) any group member can add anyone who's a friend of someone in the group. However, it is possible to set an admin approval step in group settings. Click on the drop down menu to the right of 'notifications' on the event cover and select 'edit group settings'. (Fig. 1.18)

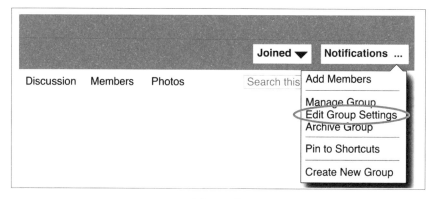

Fig 1.18

8. In group settings it is possible to:
   - Edit the group name
   - Select the type of group (choose from buy and sell, close friends, club, events and plans, family, neighbours, parents, project, schools or class, study group, support, team, travel or custom). (Fig. 1.19)
   - Choose the privacy setting for the group. This cannot be changed after the group reaches 5,000 members.

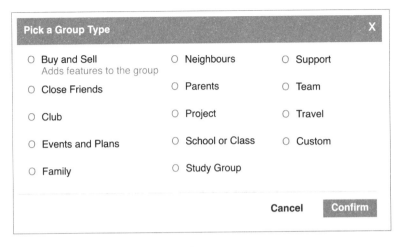

Fig 1.19

- Set the membership approval level. Choose from letting any member of the group add new members or letting any member add new members but having an admin or moderator approve them.

- Create a custom web address for the group thus making it easy to promote the group on printed material and also creating an easy to remember web address.

- Create or edit the group description and tags.

- Select who can publish posts in the group by setting post permissions. You can allow:

  ◇ Group members, moderators and admins to post in the group

  ◇ Group admins only to post in the group

  ◇ Or allow group members, moderators and admins to post in the group but all posts must be approved by an admin or moderator.

- If you set up a group you are automatically a group 'admin'. You can make other members of the group administrators by clicking into the members section on the group and selecting the icon to the right of the person's name. From there you will be able to make them an admin, moderator or remove them from the group. (Fig. 1.20)

Fig 1.20

If you make someone an administrator of the group, they will have the same control over the group as you have. They will be able to add and remove group admins and moderators, edit group settings, approve or deny membership requests, approve or deny posts in the group, remove posts and comments on posts, remove and block people from the group, pin or unpin a post in the group and view the support inbox.

Moderators can do everything an admin can except they cannot add and remove group admins and moderators or edit group settings.

1.11.2 GROUP FEATURES

Groups are different from business pages:

- Groups have 'members' rather than 'likes'.

- Group members get a notification when a post has been published in the group. This is a very useful feature. While page likes/followers may miss updates from a business page, members of groups are less likely to miss updates because of this notification.

- Any member can add their Facebook friends as new members. For some groups, depending on group settings, a group admin may need to approve their membership.

- A group member can choose to leave a group in which case they cannot be added to the group again by the group admin that initially added them.

- People can request to join a group.

- A group admin can vet new members by asking them to answer up to three questions. This lets admins screen potential members to see if they're the right fit for the group.

- It's possible to see which group members have seen each group post if the group has under 250 members. Once the group reaches this level of membership this information is no longer available.

- Facebook Insights for groups was rolled out in 2017 providing statistics on the group members and posts.

- It's possible to link your Facebook group to your business page. On your page your group will appear under the groups tab. On your group a link to your page appears on the group's cover image (see section 1.11.5).

- If your group is not linked to a business page post attribution is to the individual rather than the business page. However once a group is linked to a business page the option to post as the business page becomes available.

- Groups can be updated by writing a text post, uploading images/video, creating polls and, under the 'more' option, you can add a file, create a photo album, create a document or an event. (Figs. 1.21 and 1.22)

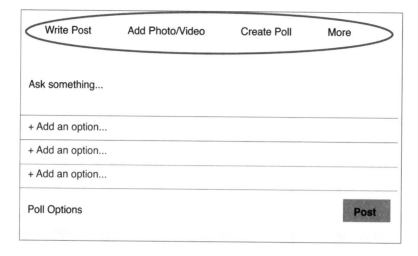

Fig 1.21

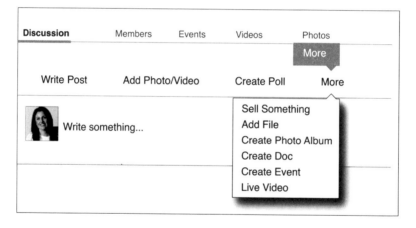

Fig 1.22

- A file can be added to the group by uploading it from your computer or from Dropbox. This is a useful way of distributing documents among group members.

- Any group member can start a group document. They can insert an image at the top, give it a title and type up the document contents. Once the document is published all group members can view and edit it. Only admins can delete documents deleted by others. This is a great way of sharing information and ideas in the group. (Fig. 1.23)

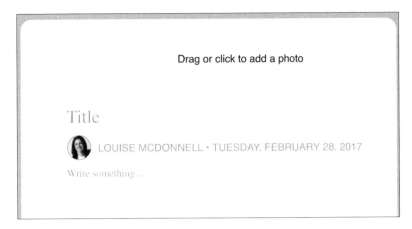

Fig 1.23

1.11.3 TYPES OF GROUPS

Groups can be public, closed or secret depending on their privacy settings. Groups of under 5,000 members can change their privacy settings at any time. After this it is not possible to change.

Public Groups

Anyone can join or be added or invited by a member. The group will show up in Facebook and Google searches and anyone will be able to see the group's name, description, members and posts.

Closed Groups

Anyone can ask to join or be added or invited by a group member. The group will show up in Facebook searches and anyone can see the group's name and description, however only group members can see group members and the group posts.

Secret Groups

Anyone can join a secret group, but they have to be added or invited by a group member. The group will only appear in Facebook search to current and former members and only current and formers group members can see the group's name and description. Only current members see group members and posts.

1.11.4 HOW BUSINESSES CAN USE GROUPS

I have found secret groups to be useful for simplifying communications between committee members. This is particularly useful for community groups or charities where members of committees or sub-committees are volunteers who don't live or work in close proximity to each other. A secret group is secure as no one other than group members will know of its existence as it can't be found in Facebook searches. Any posts published in the group are only seen by group members. So all group conversations are completely private. It's also possible to see who has seen each post published in the group.

Similarly, a secret group is a secure and convenient way to communicate with staff members, particularly if there are part time or shift staff. Businesses can also easily see who has seen updates posted in the group (as long as the group has less than 250 members).

Businesses can set up an exclusive group for customers for specific products or services. Any business that charges customers to be part of a club, programme or service it is offering could consider using a secret or closed group. Fitness professionals have used this very effectively. People sign up to a fitness programme and are then given access to a closed or secret group. Once the programme is over, or they cancel their subscription, they are removed from the group. Other businesses that have used this successfully include social media experts, business coaches, life coaches, etc.

Groups like this tend to be closed. They will show up in a Facebook search and the group cover image and description will be public, but the group posts are not visible. It's a useful way for businesses to let potential customers know that their group exists but only subscribers benefit from the updates. As anyone can post updates, not just the business owner, group members can provide peer support and in doing so create a sense of community.

Setting up a public group, which is open to anyone to see, is another way businesses can encourage potential customers to connect with them. My group 'Facebook Marketing with LouiseMcD' is an example of this type of group. I post tips and advice related to Facebook marketing. I find it useful for reaching out to new members and warming up cold prospects.

Sales groups tend to be used by groups of businesses in a sector. For example, a network of craft businesses could set up a sales group. This creates a 'marketplace' as anyone in the group can post items for sale and members of the public know that by joining this group they can find this type of product. Sales groups are also popular with individuals selling second hand items.

1.11.5 How to Link a Facebook Group to a Facebook Page

Link your Facebook page to your group under the 'edit page' section under 'settings'. Add 'groups' as a tab to your page. (Fig. 1.24)

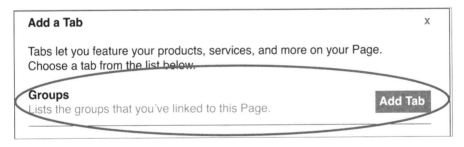

Fig 1.24

Then exit the settings section and click into the groups tab on your page. Select from there which group you wish to link to your page. (Fig. 1.25)

When you link your Facebook group to your Facebook page:

- A link to the group appears in the tabs section of your page
- A link to your page appears at the top of your group
- You will be able to post, comment and react to posts on your groups as your page.

47

Build Community Around Your Page

Build community around your business, brand or organisation with groups. You can interact with people in your groups as your Page, and your Page can be an admin of these groups.

Create Group   **Link your Group**

Fig 1.25

1.12 FACEBOOK EVENTS

Anyone who has ever organised an event will understand the challenges involved: setting the event time and date, raising awareness, inviting attendees, collating RSVPs, building excitement ahead of the event and reminding people to attend.

Facebook Events offer organisers support with every aspect of marketing events. It is a very practical marketing tool that assists people to organise and promote events.

1.12.1 HOW TO SET UP A FACEBOOK EVENT

Events can be set up from a business page, Facebook group or an individual. Events created by individuals can be private or public. For private events you can invite your Facebook friends to attend your event. You also have the option of allowing your friends to invite people. Only those invited to the event will see it. Individuals can also create public events which are visible to everyone, even people they are not 'friends' with on Facebook.

Set up an event from a business page by selecting the dropdown menu at the top of the page. (Figs. 1.26 and 1.27)

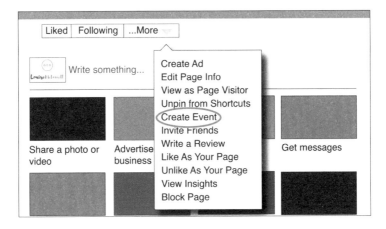

Fig 1.26

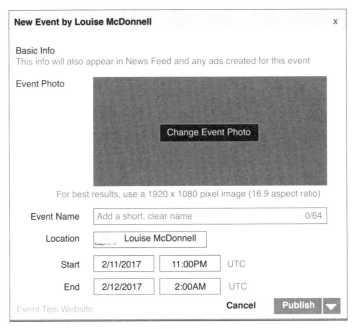

Fig 1.27

Select an event image that represents your event. For best results across desktop and mobile platforms, Facebook suggest using a 1920 x 1080 pixel image (16:9 aspect ratio). Images with little or no text perform better in Facebook ads.

Choose a short, clear name. Avoid including the event location name or unnecessary or irrelevant words like 'official' or 'for one night only' in the event title. If your name is too long it may be truncated. Keep your event name clear and simple and avoid using block letters or symbols as they are difficult to read.

Use a location that corresponds to a Facebook page or a Facebook location if possible. Facebook will suggest the event (public events) to people nearby through suggestions.

Set a time and date. Set a specific date and time so that it is clear to attendees when the event is taking place. If your event is running longer than a two week period Facebook recommends creating separate events.

In the event description, tell people why they should attend. What can you say in the first sentence to capture their attention? Why will the event be of interest to them? Remember, it's not about why *you're* holding the event, it's about why *they* should attend. Include the event schedule, tag other relevant pages and public profiles and use relevant hastags.

Associate keywords with your event that will assist Facebook index it for relevant searches (for public events) and will help people learn quickly what your event is about.

If you are selling tickets for your event you can add a link to the website where tickets can be purchased.

If you are working with other organisations like sponsors, stakeholders or suppliers include them as co-hosts to your event. This will enable them to add the event to their calendars and to invite their fans to attend. Co-hosts can also edit the event.

You can set who can post on the event page. You can allow anyone to post, allow anyone to post but a host must approve it before it appears or just limit posts to hosts only.

It's possible to show or hide the guest list. (Fig 1.28)

You can save drafts of the event, which will be visible to all event admins before the event is published. Drafts are found under the events tab on your page.

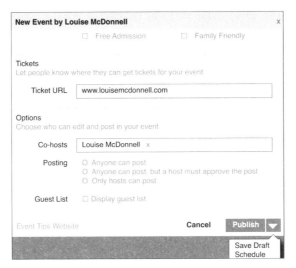

Fig 1.28

Once you have completed setting up the event you can publish it or schedule it to be published at a future date and time. You can edit the event after it is published. If your event has a large number of responses you are limited to changing the time and location to three times. After the event begins you will no longer be able to edit event details.

If you are regularly running similar events, you can set up new ones by duplicating past events. Select the 'more' dropdown menu on your event page and update the relevant fields before publishing or scheduling.

Facebook is now working closely with ticketing companies like Eventbrite and Ticketmaster to integrate the ability to purchase and access tickets on Facebook (the user does not have to leave Facebook and go to an external site to purchase or access tickets). This is referred to as API integration.

1.12.2 HOW TO PROMOTE YOUR FACEBOOK EVENT

1. Invite your Facebook friends to attend. You can select the friends to which the event will be relevant.

2. Encourage everyone who is working with you on the event to invite their friends.

3. Share the event on your Facebook pages and groups. The 'share' button is found under the event cover image on the top right hand side. You can share the event on your page, in your group, on your own timeline or with people you select in Facebook messenger. Think about the timing of this. If you have invited your friends to attend, leave it a day or so before sharing on your own timeline/pages. (Fig. 1.29)

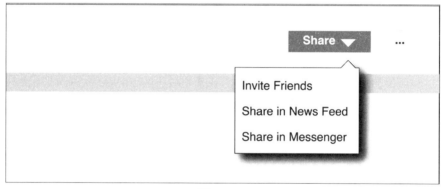

Fig 1.29

4. Encourage all co-hosts, sponsors and stakeholders to share the event on their pages and groups and to encourage people to attend.

5. Post regular updates on the event timeline. Anyone who has accepted the invitation to attend the event will be notified when you post an update. How can you build excitement about the event? Can you drip feed a line-up of performers or speakers? Can you run a competition? Can you publish interesting facts or statistics?

6. Use Facebook Live at your event to build excitement and to engage your audience before, during or after the event.

7. Use Facebook Ads to promote your event. Run campaigns to increase awareness about the event before and after the event launch.

8. Remarket to customer databases like your customer list, attendees of past events, page fans, website visitors and people that have watched event videos or live broadcasts. Reach new people from your target audience by choosing lookalike or saved audiences (see section 5.2 for more information).

9. Increase awareness through boosting posts from the event page, or creating a landing page on your website with lead magnet like a cheat sheet/handout, free industry report, toolkit/resource list, free training, free trial, etc.

10. Use Engagement Ads to increase event responses. This type of ad is optimised to get as many people as possible from the target audience to attend your event. Target warm audiences with consideration and conversion campaigns.

11. Use Facebook Ads Manager to create 'traffic' and 'conversion' ads driving traffic to a web page where event tickets can be purchased. While traffic ads are optimised for link clicks, conversion ads are optimised for sales conversions. You will need to have the Facebook pixel on your webpage to run conversion ads. See Chapter 5 on Facebook Ads for more information and planning and running Facebook ad campaigns.

12. Promote your events on your other social media platforms and in your email marketing campaigns, linking back to your Facebook Event page to encourage sign ups.

1.12.4 MEASURING PERFORMANCE

Use event insights to understand how your events have performed. Use awareness, engagement, ticketing and audience insights to get to know your customers and customise ad targeting.

Awareness

This gives a timeline of when people from your target audience saw your event page. Use this to learn what promotional activity had an impact with your audience. The information in this tab is broken down between 'people reached' and 'event page views'. (Fig 1.30)

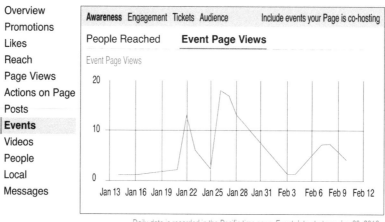

Fig 1.30

Engagement

In this tab learn when your audience responded when they saw your event or visited the event page. (Fig. 1.31)

Tickets

Find out when your audience purchased event tickets. See when people purchased event tickets. Did this correspond to posts published on the event page, or boosted posts or Facebook ads? Tuning into this will assist with future campaigns.

Audience

Learn more about the demographics of people who attended your event. What was the breakdown of age profile and gender? This can assist with creating or tweaking your saved audience for future Facebook ads. (Fig. 1.32)

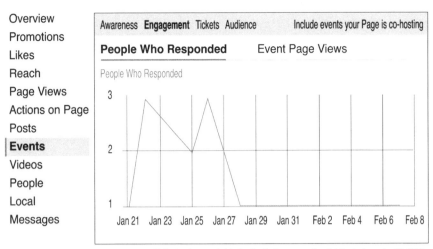

Fig 1.31

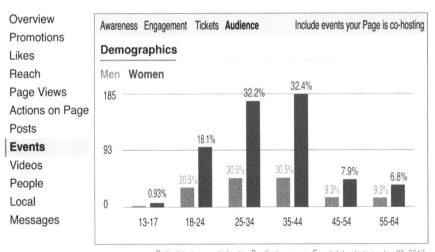

Fig 1.32

1.13 SETTING SMART GOALS

Whether you are setting up a new page or want to improve the performance of an existing one, you should set medium- to long-terms goals to stay focused.

SMART goals are goals that are Specific, Measurable – which usually means they have a number associated with them – Achievable – there is no point in having a goal that you have no hope in achieving – Realistic and with a Timeframe associated with them.

Below are some examples of SMART goals for your business page.

1. How Many Page Likes by a Certain Date

If you're a small business in a rural area you'll have a different goal for page likes than an ecommerce store targeting customers nationally or internationally. My advice is to check out your competition and set a goal with a specific timeframe in mind.

Remember, it's better to grow page likes with people who are genuinely interested in your business. Don't ask people to like your page for the sake of it. If they're not interested in your products and services they will never engage with your posts and they'll never buy anything from you.

2. Post Engagements

When people engage with your posts (click, like, comment or share) Facebook knows they are interested in your page. As a result they are more likely to show more of your posts to them in the future. So being conscious of achieving high engagement levels will assist with the organic reach of your page, that is, the number of people that see your posts or the non-paid traffic (see section 7 for statistics on post engagements).

3. Weekly Page Reach

The weekly reach of your page relates to the number of people who see your posts. The more you post and the better the quality of your posts the higher your reach will be. So be conscious of what your weekly reach is and put a SMART goal in place that will motivate you to improve this metric (see section 7.1 for statistics on page reach).

3. Enquiries Emanating from Facebook (email, comments to page or private messages)

If it is important to generate enquires through your page and setting a goal around this will keep you focused. You will also need to consider what content you need to produce to encourage email signups/enquiries.

4. Email Signups

If building an email list is important set a goal relating to this on your Facebook page.

5. Referral Traffic to Your Website

If you have a website or ecommerce store and you are using Google Analytics – you should check to see how much traffic is coming from Facebook. The more active your page is and the more links you share from your website the higher this figure will be.

Once you have set your goals and developed a strategy to achieve them this will influence the content you push out on your page (see Chapter 3).

SET SMART GOALS

1. The current Facebook page likes are ____. I would like to grow this to ____ by (date) ____.

2. The goal I would like to set for page performance is ____ people reached in the next 7 days.

3. Goal for enquiries emanating (email, comments to page or private messages) is _____.

4. Email signups goal is _____.

5. Referral traffic to my website goal is _____.

6. My campaign goals are _____.

1.14 TEN POINT CHECKLIST FOR YOUR FACEBOOK PAGE

---

1. Are you using your logo or professional head shot as your profile picture? Remember that your profile picture is used as the thumbnail that appears alongside your posts in the news feed. This is important for raising brand awareness (see sections 1.5 and 3.8 for more info).

2. Is your cover image a good representation of your business? It can be seasonal or used to highlight different campaigns. Integrating brand colours will make your page look professional. Consider using one of the slider images from your website to help people make a connection between it and your page. Use a video Facebook cover to really impress page fans (see sections 1.5 and 3.8 for more info).

3. Have you claimed your username? Inserting your username after www.Facebook.com/creates a vanity URL to your Facebook page. My username is LouiseMcDSocial so I use www.Facebook.com/LouiseMcDSocial to direct people to my page. I use this address on email signatures, business cards, brochures and during interviews (see sections 1.5 and 1.8 for more info).

4. Have you set up your 'call to action' button on your page? Prompt people to take action by making it obvious what

you want them to do next. Do you want them to call you, visit your website, download your app, make a donation, book services etc. (see section 1.8 for more info).

5. Have your turned page messaging on? Make it easy for people to start a conversation with you. Respond quickly to messages to earn a 'responsive' badge from Facebook (see 1.7 for more info).

6. Have you set a featured video? Select one of your native videos to be featured at the top of your page. It will be one of the first things people who visit your page will see. Set this up under the video tab.

7. Have you organised your page tabs? Reorder your tabs to highlight your strong points. If you have lots of 5 star reviews, then consider moving this tab to the top. If you have a library of high quality native videos, give the video tab a prominent position on your page. Turn off out of date tabs that no longer function (for example, page welcome tabs). Set up custom tabs like, email sign up forms or contest forms (see section 1.7 for more info).

8. Have you set up the Facebook shop to sell products or services? Create shop tab under the edit page section under settings. Businesses with ecommerce stores can link Facebook shop products to the corresponding page on their website. Businesses without ecommerce stores can take transactions offline (see section 1.7 for more info).

9. Can customers leave reviews on your page? Let potential customers know what your current customers think about you! Encourage 5 star reviews by asking satisfied customers to post reviews. Repond carefully to any negative reviews (see section 1.8.1 for more info).

10. Publish high quality content regularly on your page. Create content that will resonate with your target audiences. Integrate your visual identity to reinforce brand identity. Let visitors to your page know what's happening in your business right now. Having an active page with great content is one of the best ways of impressing customers and potential customers (see Chapter 3).

Chapter 2

CUSTOMER ANALYSIS AND PROFILING

2.1 LEARNING ABOUT YOUR CUSTOMERS

Understanding your customers is the key to running a successful Facebook page. It will enable you to identify key audiences, create content that will appeal to them and run more effective Facebook ad campaigns.

Customers are the lifeline of every business. Businesses that understand their customers' needs, wants and motivations clearly have a better chance of succeeding than those that don't. They are better at product development, selecting distribution channels, pricing and marketing. In order to understand your customers you need to consider the following questions:

- Who are your customers?
- What are their needs?
- Do you meet those needs?
- Are they satisfied with your product/service offering?
- How can you reach your customers?
- What will you say to them to encourage them to buy (more) from you?

According to Bain & Co, it is six to seven times more expensive to gain a new customer than to retain an existing one. Existing customers also spend 67 per cent more and after 10 purchases have referred up to seven people.

According to *Understanding Customers* by Ruby Newell-Legner:

- For every customer who complains, 26 remain silent.
- It takes 12 positive incidents to make up for 1 negative one.
- The average 'wronged customer' will tell 8 to 16 people.
- Over 20 per cent will tell more than 20 others.
- 91 per cent of unhappy customers will not willingly return.
- 70 per cent of complaining customers will repeat their business if you resolve the complaint in their favour.
- 95 per cent of complaining customers will do business with you again if you resolve the complaint instantly.
- A typical business hears from 4 per cent of dissatisfied customers.

There are some simple exercises that any business can carry out with the aim of gaining a better understanding about its customers.

2.1.1 BRAINSTORMING

Small business owners are often so busy trying to run their businesses that they haven't taken the time to consider why customers do business with them. What makes you different from your competitors? What makes you unique? You may vaguely know, but have never written it down and if pushed couldn't quickly make an 'elevator pitch', that is, in a short period of time to pitch to your ideal customer.

Brainstorming is great because there are no right or wrong answers, the idea is to write everything down. I recommend trying to make the session as informal as possible. If you are a small business with employees, invite them to take 30 minutes out of their day, bring in some coffee and pastries and let the creative juices flow! If you're a solopreneur why not sit down with a friend, partner or someone who knows you and your business?

Feedback may not be instant, but that's okay. Allow people time to warm up and encourage participation by acknowledging every suggestion and writing it down.

Here are some questions to consider using:

- When people hear what you do, what questions do they ask?
- What does your ideal customer complain about?
- What problems do you solve?
- What needs do your products/services meet?
- Think about three of your most loyal customers and consider why they like doing business with you.
- Think about a time recently when a potential customer enquired but did not do business with you. Why did you lose this business?

2..1.2 Customer Chat

A second way of researching about your customers is to simply have an informal chat with two or three. You could meet for coffee or simply chat over the phone. Don't assume that your customer has time to talk to you when they're in your place of business.

Choose a customer who will be honest and objective. For this reason avoid chatting to really good friends or family. Keep your chat informal so your customer feels relaxed and comfortable. This is a listening exercise, so be prepared to ask questions and then just listen. If there is a silence, give your customers time to think and process their answer. They will eventually fill the silence. Don't challenge negative feedback. It may discourage any further criticism. Remember, the goal of the exercise is to understand your customers better. If they have misconceptions about your business it's better to find out what they are. You can always deal with their mistaken views at some time in the future.

2.1.3 FOCUS GROUPS

A focus group is a small group of six to ten people led through an open discussion by a skilled moderator. Before running the focus group, set out clearly the objectives of the session. What do you want to achieve by running this focus group?

The moderator should be neutral and should have a clear understanding of the set objectives.

During the session people should be encouraged to discuss topics freely. The session should be between about 45 to 90 minutes in duration. Begin the session with the most important questions.

The group needs to be large enough to generate rich discussion but not so large that some participants are left out.

2.1.4 CUSTOMER SURVEYS

Conducting a customer survey is something every business can easily carry out and it can assist in profiling customers. Customers can be profiled by demographic factors such as age, sex, education level, income level, marital status, occupation, religion, average size of a family. Demographics tell you *who* your customers are. Another way to profile customers is by psychographic profiling. Psychographics explain *why* customers buy from you and takes into consideration buyers' habits, hobbies and values.

Understanding who your customers are and why they choose to do business with you can provide useful information for finding new customers. While this is a fundamental tactic of marketing in general, it is particularly useful for Facebook as you can use demographic profiling to tell Facebook who your ideal customer is (preferred audiences), create audiences in Facebook ads and use psychographic profiling to produce content on your page that resonates with your target audience.

When carrying out your survey I recommend using SurveyMonkey, a web-based survey software company. The software is free to use if you have under 10 questions and under 100 respondents. Beyond that there are monthly packages that you can select depending on your survey.

There are a number of steps I recommend following when doing your customer survey:

1. Establish what the survey's goals are. What do you want to achieve? How are you planning to use the information that you are gathering? If you wish to establish demographic and psychographic profiles what questions should you include?

2. Use simple language avoiding jargon and industry acronyms. Respondents are more likely to abandon surveys if they don't understand the questions.

3. Closed questions, giving respondents specific choices (for example, multiple choice or yes/no) make it easier to analyse survey results.

4. Open-ended questions allow respondents to answer questions in their own words. It offers the opportunity to express opinions that you might not have factored into multiple choice answers. Although it is more difficult to analyze results from open-ended questions, they can play an important part in psychographic profiling.

5. Keep rating scale questions consistent throughout the survey to avoid confusing respondents. When creating questions with rating scales using an odd number will make data analysis easier (for example, 1 = very dissatisfied and 5 = very satisfied). Use this rating consistently throughout the survey.

6. Order your questions in a way that is logical and that will motivate respondents to complete the survey. Begin your survey with a brief introduction. Thank respondents for completing it, explain who you are, why you are conducting the survey, how many questions there are and how long it should take to complete. Start with questions that everyone will find easy to answer and introduce harder questions later in the survey.

7. Consider whether you wish to allow respondents to remain anonymous. People may be more inclined to give negative feedback in this instance.

8. Once you have finished the survey design, it's always a good idea to pre-test it with a handful of respondents. This will show up any problems with the survey such as misinterpretation of questions or issues analysing data.

9. Encourage responses by:
   ◇ Emailing your customer list
   ◇ Texting your customer list
   ◇ Publishing a link on your Facebook page
   ◇ Publishing a link on other social media channels
   ◇ Posting a link to the survey on your website
   ◇ Leaving hard copies of your survey in your place of business or at company events.

What can you hope to establish?
- Customer demographics
- How customers heard about you
- How satisfied customers are
- Gaps in your offerings
- How they booked with you
- How far in advance they have booked

- If different customer profiles have different perceptions/ requirements
- What social networks your customers use
- How frequently they use social media
- Whether they have made appointments/enquiries using social media
- Whether they have visited your website.

2.1.5 FACEBOOK INSIGHTS

Consult Facebook Insights to learn more about who is connecting with your page on Facebook. The insights section is found on the top administration panel on your page. Select the 'people tab' to see a breakdown of the age, gender and location of your fans. You can also get a breakdown of the people your page has reached and who have engaged (liked, commented, shared, clicked) with your posts (see section 7.11).

2.1.6 AUDIENCE INSIGHTS

Once you have over 1,000 fans you can use Facebook Ads Audience Insights to learn more about the profiles of people who 'like' or 'follow' your page. Audience Insights is a tool found in Facebook Ads Manager. (see Figs. 2.1 and 2.2)

Although this tool was developed to assist advertisers to target their ads more effectively, it can also be used to learn more about the profile of your fans.

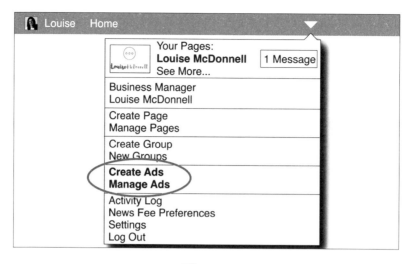

Fig. 2.1

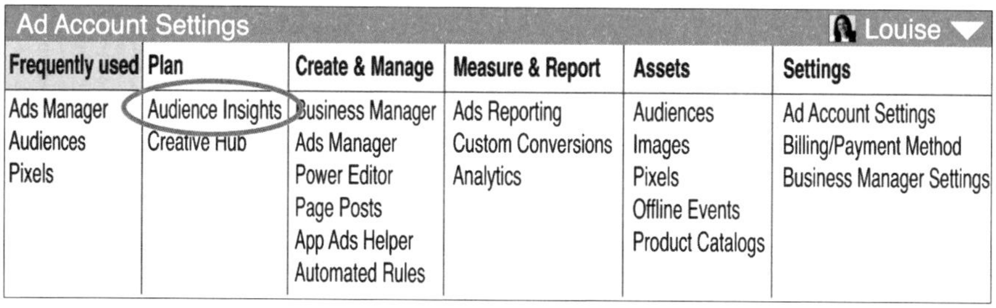

Fig. 2.2

Facebook Insights enables you to analyse different audiences on Facebook by:

- Age and gender
- Relationship status
- Education level
- Job title
- Other pages they have liked
- Location by country, city
- Language
- Activity on Facebook
- Devices used on Facebook.

Use the panel on the left hand side to select an audience you wish to analyse. You can select by:

- Country
- Interest
- Connections
- Behaviours on Facebook. (Fig. 2.3)

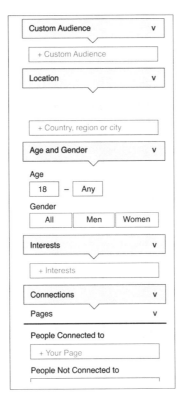

Fig. 2.3

In the 'by connections' dialogue box type in the name of your Facebook business page to analyse the characteristics of your fans. Only Facebook page admins have this option (so it's not possible to use this tool to analyse the fans of competitors' pages). The more fans you have the more Facebook can draw similarities in their characteristics.

2.2 DEVELOPING BUYER PERSONAS

Buyer personas describe the individuals and groups of people who buy your products or services. They are your typical customers. A persona needs to be created for each customer group.

Use the information you have gathered as part of your primary (brainstorming, customer interviews, customer survey) and secondary (Facebook insights, audience insights, information from you internal business management tools) market research to create personas.

Give each persona a name and use a photograph which typifies this customer. Use questions like:

- Age and gender?
- Where do they live?
- Where do they work?
- What do they do to de-stress?
- Where do they shop?
- What do they read?
- What radio stations do they listen to?
- What social networks do they use?
- How can you make their lives easier?

By creating a profile of your typical customer it makes it easy to 'speak to them'. It assists with all aspects of marketing your business including writing website content, choosing appropriate images, sales pitches, ad copy, content for your Facebook page and how to publish posts that they are likely to engage with.

2.2.1 PERSONA EXAMPLE

Here is an example of a customer persona using the audience insights from Charlene Flanagan Makeup's Page. (Fig. 2.4)

Name: Aoife Occupation: Sales/Admin Age: 27 (between 24-34)	
Location	Ireland
Education Level	3rd Level
Relationship Status	In a relationship
Where she likes to shop	Asos, Pennys, H&M
Other pages she likes	Pippa O'Connor, So Sue Me
What I know about this persona	This persona responds well to practical tips. They tend to be very interested in skincare, contouring and eye makeup. Shorter videos under three minutes work best. This is the best persona for wedding makeup sales and sales of masterclass tutorials.

Fig. 2.4

Rachel represents Charlene's typical customer. When coming up with content ideas for her page, Charlene should think about Rachel, maybe stick a picture of Rachel beside her PC and attempt to walk in Rachel's shoes.

- What is Rachel interested in?
- What's going in in her life?
- What type of questions does Rachel typically ask?
- If Charlene was doing a makeup lesson for Rachel what would she be most interested in?
- What images will catch Rachel's attention?
- What content has she engaged with in the past?

When it comes to content creation the focus must be on your customers. Don't just tell customers what *you* do, tell them how *they* will benefit.

2.2.2 Four Reasons to Use Customer Personas for Facebook Marketing

Using a customer-centric approach to content marketing helps in a number of ways:

1. Your content will be more relevant to your customer. It will endear them to your brand and encourage them to do business with you as they will believe that you understand them better.

2. The posts on your page will have a higher organic reach. When your fans engage (like, comment, share, click) with a post on your page Facebook knows the content is good and shows it to more of your fans. Facebook also knows that fans who engage with your page must like your content and are therefore more likely to show them more of your future posts.

3. Posts on your page will be seen by friends of fans of your page. If a fan finds a post on a page particularly useful they may share it with their friends or tag specific ones. In this way you are reaching beyond your existing fan base.

4. You will get a better return from boosted posts. A boosted post (see more in Chapter 5) is where you pay Facebook to show a post on your page to an audience you select. If you boost a post to your ideal customer (in our example above, to an audience that matches Rachel's persona) and the content appeals to them, they are more likely to engage with the post, like your page and share the content with their friends, thus kick starting a further organic reach.

2.3 THE CUSTOMER LOYALTY LADDER AND SOCIAL MEDIA

As noted earlier, customers will buy from you when *they* are ready to buy, not when *you* are ready to sell. Once you acknowledge this and identify that there are different types of customers it will change the way you approach social media.

2.3.1 DISINTERESTED

These are potential customers who simply do not have a need for what you are selling at the moment. You are not on their radar. In this instance they will probably not notice your Facebook posts, page or any other marketing you carry out such as newspaper ads, road signs and so on. However, there is always that chance if they match the demographic profiling of your customers that in the future this may change.

2.3.2 SUSPECT

This is someone who is beginning to become aware of a need for what you are selling. At this stage they may notice your Facebook posts and page, but it's unlikely that they will like your page or engage with your posts. They may, however, start to notice your posts.

2.3.3 PROSPECT

A prospect has identified that they have a requirement for a product or a service you are offering. At this stage they are evaluating their options. Prospects are more likely to 'like' your page. They will potentially check out the 'about us' section and from there your website. That's why it's so important to communicate your unique selling position effectively in your company description as well as on your website. They will be interested in reviews on your page, as this is what others are saying about you. They'll also look through the most recent posts to see what's happening in your business. They may send a private message to your page to seek a quote from you or to start a conversation about a potential sale. Remember, prospects are potentially contacting your competitors too, so just because they have a requirement for what you sell doesn't mean they will convert.

2.3.4 CUSTOMERS

Customers are prospects who have converted. There is a high likelihood that they 'like' your page and they may start engaging with your posts. The degree to which they engage is dependent on how satisfied they are with you and how relevant the content on your page is.

2.3.5 ADVOCATES

Loyal customers who are extremely satisfied with your company have the potential to become 'raving fans'. They are so happy with you that they refer you to their friends, family and associates. Raving fans are extremely likely to 'like' your page and to engage with your posts. They like you so much they are very likely to share your Facebook posts, post reviews on your page and add positive comments to your posts.

When you publish a post on your Facebook page you are potentially reaching people who are disinterested, suspects, prospects, customers and advocates.

Rather than seeing Facebook as a place where you can sell, you should see it as a place where you can connect with potential customers. The aim is to consistently get your brand in front of people who are likely to have a requirement for what you are offering so that when they become a prospect they consider doing business with you.

2.4 QUALIFYING AUDIENCES

Another way to think about the audiences you can reach through Facebook is to consider how 'warm' they are to your brand. The most common mistake businesses make on Facebook is that they try to sell to cold audiences. People who have never heard about your company, its products or services, even if they match the profile of your ideal customer, rarely convert.

2.4.1 COLD AUDIENCES

Although these people don't know your brand, if they match the profile of your ideal customer they are likely to be interested in your content. Again, don't try to sell to cold audiences. Instead, aim to introduce them to your brand and raise awareness by creating attractive content on your page.

Encourage cold audiences to:

- Like or follow your page. Once you have them as a page like, you have the opportunity to reach them organically every time you publish a post on your page.

- Engage with the posts on your page. Encourage prospects who have liked (reacted) to one of the posts on your page to like your page by clicking the 'invite' option beside their names. Click on the link underneath the post which lists the names of the people who have liked it. Then invite people who have liked the post but are not fans of your page to become fans. (Fig. 2.5)

- Watch your videos. In Chapter 5 I'll be showing you how you can re-market (re-target) people who have watched your videos. Remember, people are more likely to watch a video if the content is relevant and helpful to them.

- Read your blogs. Getting a cold prospect to read a blog article that solves a problem or provides useful advice is a great way of introducing them to your brand.

Fig. 2.5

2.4.2 WARM AUDIENCES

Warm audiences are people who already know about you, your brand, products or services. They have seen your page and the posts you have published. They may have watched some of your videos or read some of your blog articles.

How 'warm' they are depends on how much your brand has impressed them.

Warm prospects are more likely to do business with you than cold prospects. Your job as a marketeer is to keep getting your brand in front of warm prospects so that when they have a requirement for what you are offering they consider doing business with you.

Targeting sales posts and ads to warmer audiences will lead to higher conversion rates.

2.4.3 HOT AUDIENCES

These are existing customers who like your brand. They have had their expectations met or exceeded when they have done business with you in the past and are therefore more likely to repeat business with you in the future. The more you have exceeded their expectations the more likely they are to reengage with you and to recommend you to others.

2.5 BUILDING A SALES FUNNEL USING FACEBOOK

So you've done the research and have created your customer personas. You have identified that there are different types of customers on the loyalty ladder. In this section we are going to consider how you can marry the two. How can you use this information to start creating a winning strategy for your Facebook page?

By creating a sales funnel you will see how you can move customers along the loyalty ladder with the ultimate aim of making them customer advocates.

There are six stages in the sales funnel.

1. Attract Quality Likes to Your Page

Not all likes are the same. You should only aim to attract page likes from people who have the potential to become customers. Asking people to like your page for the sake of it is of no real benefit. Similarly, running competitions or contests may only attract people who are interested in winning the prize, even if they will never have a need for you what you sell. People like this are unlikely to ever engage with your content because they aren't interested in it. Focus instead on attracting better quality likes. Use your customer personas to target people who are likely to become customers. There are a number of ways to do this:

- Set your ideal audience in your page settings (audience optimisation for posts)
- Create content that will appeal to your target audience. Posts that solve a problem or offer advice will earn you trust with a cold prospect.

- Boost posts (create sponsored stories) to audiences that fit the profile of your ideal customer

- Launch campaigns to grow page likes.

2. Warm Them Up

Once you have attracted likes to your page that have potential to become customers, your next challenge is to warm them up. This can be done by consistently publishing content that is relevant to them and that they find useful. Solve a problem for them and you will begin to earn their trust. Respond to their comments and questions and you will start to build a relationship with them. Don't attempt to sell to them before you have warmed them up as you may risk frightening them away.

3. Build a Database

Encourage your likes to subscribe to your customer lists. Aim to collect email addresses or mobile numbers. Remember, you don't own your Facebook page and you can't control what will happen with it in the future or how you will communicate with your audience. But you do own your customer list. You have full control over when and how you contact your subscribers. A good way to encourage your fans to subscribe to your customer list is to offer them something of value like a free fact sheet, a free video tutorial, a discount code or a free consultation. You will find that the fans who are the most interested in your products are most likely to subscribe. You have moved them along your funnel.

4. Generate Leads

When you have identified your warmest prospects you can then start to sell to them. You can email them, post on your Facebook page and target them directly with Facebook ads. Conversions can be tracked using Facebook conversion ads.

5. Convert

Only prospects that are 'warm' to your brand are likely to convert. Target your sales posts at your warmest fans. These are people who already like your page, have watched your videos on Facebook, have engaged with the posts on your page, have subscribed to your mailing list and have visited your website.

6. Delight

Create delighted customers by not just meeting their expectations but exceeding them. Delighted customers are more likely to refer new prospects to your sales funnel. Delighted customers will happily engage with the posts on your page, are more likely to share content from your page, watch your videos and attend your events. Encourage customers who are 'raving' about your brand to post a review on your Facebook page.

Chapter 3

CREATING HIGH QUALITY CONTENT

Understanding your customers is the key to successful content creation on Facebook. In the last chapter we investigated who your customers are and considered the reasons they do business with you. Having done some research into customer demographics and psychographics we created customer personas. In this section we are going to start 'having conversations' with your personas. We are going to visualise your typical customers and what you would say to them if they were sitting in front of you.

Social media is about connecting with your audience and consistently communicating your core values to them.

Think of your Facebook page as a radio station where your customers can tune in. What would you broadcast to keep them interested? Would you tune into a radio station that broadcast nothing but ads? Well neither will your customers. If you publish one sales post after another your audience will tune out. In Chapter 1 we discussed the Facebook algorithm, Edgerank, which controls what appears on Facebook. If people who like your page stop engaging (liking, commenting, clicking, sharing) with posts on your page, there is a high likelihood that Facebook will stop showing your posts to them. It presumes they're not interested. And they probably aren't!

The most important advice when it comes to creating content for your Facebook page is ... *it's not about what you want to say, it's about what your customer wants to hear from you. It's not about you. It's about them.*

If you publish content that is useful to your customer they are much more likely to engage.

3.1 WHY PEOPLE ENGAGE

3.1.1 WHY PEOPLE 'REACT' (LIKE) POSTS

People can associate a range of emotions with a Facebook post. (See Fig. 3.1). They can choose from the following: Like, Love, Ha Ha, Wow, Sad, Angry.

Fig. 3.1

People will associate their emotions with a post to:

- Acknowledge that they have seen it
- Show support
- Let others know what they think.

You need to remember that people are flicking quickly through their news feed. They may stop and look at your posts but not click the 'like' button. They are not thinking about how they can keep you happy by 'liking' your post. Remember ... *it's not about you, it's about them.*

You can encourage people to like your posts by simply asking them: 'Like this post to show your support' or 'Like this post if you agree with …'. Or 'Like this post to congratulate …'.

3.1.2 WHY FANS 'COMMENT' ON POSTS

People comment on posts to:

- Express their opinion, whether they agree or disagree
- Let their friends know what they think
- To raise their profile with your audience – comments on your posts are visible to everyone
- Tag friends who they know will be interested in the post.

It's hard to get people to comment. They have to think about what they are going to say and then spend time typing it. If your page only has a few hundred likes avoid publishing too many posts where you ask people to comment. One tactic to encourage comments is to ask some of your friends to comment which may in turn encourage others to do so.

The more emotive the subject the more likely people are to comment. People will regularly tag friends in posts to draw their attention to them. Publishing high quality content that is useful to the reader will encourage this. (Fig. 3.2)

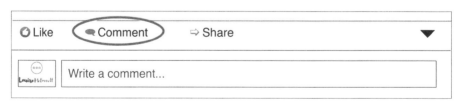

Fig. 3.2

3.1.3 WHY PEOPLE SHARE POSTS

When people share posts it goes into their news feed and therefore has the potential to reach all of their Facebook friends. In terms of engagement it's the crème de la crème. It's the most cost effective way of extending the organic reach of your page, that is, the number of people who see your posts without you having to pay.

People will share posts if they:

- Think the information contained in the post is so good that they want all their friends to see it
- Are a brand advocate (see section 2.3) and want to tell everyone they know about your products/services
- Believe in a cause and want to influence their friends
- Want to let their friends know what they think about a particular subject.

The people most likely to share your posts are your friends, family and brand advocates. Beyond this, people will share your posts if they are so impressed with the content that they want others to see it. (Fig. 3.3)

Fig. 3.3

3.1.4 CLICKING ON POSTS

Getting someone to click on your posts is the easiest form of engagement. There is no commitment on your readers' part. They are not seen to be publicly endorsing your content.

If they are interested and want to find out more, they will simply click on your post without giving it too much thought. The simple 'click' is often overlooked by business page owners, but it is the simplest and most effective way to get visitors to your page to interact with your posts.

People will click on posts to:

- Click on links contained in your posts (links to websites)
- Visit other pages you have tagged
- View multiple images or a video
- 'See more' if your post contains a lot of text.

3.2 CONTENT CREATION

When it comes to content creation, you need to continually ask yourself, 'What do my customers want to hear from me?' Remember, people are more likely to engage with a post if it is of interest to them.

It's not about what you want to say – it's about what they want to hear.

That's where most business pages fall down. They post one sales pitch after another. This happens when people don't plan their posts, have no strategy in place and are just posting on their page for the sake of posting.

A woman told me recently that she posted a review on a barber's Facebook page as she was delighted with their service. She had brought her 16-year-old son to have his hair cut. When he emerged a while later he was like a new person. He was blown away with the service. The stylist had taken the time to talk to him about his hair style, had explained what would work and what wouldn't and had then proceeded to restyle his hair. He felt like a million dollars. The whole atmosphere in the family home was transformed because of this experience.

So what were the benefits for this lady for using this service? Happiness, confidence, harmony at home for the evening. So much more than she or her son had expected.

People will rarely remember what you did or said, but they will always remember how you made them feel.

When you exceed customers' expectations, you 'delight' them. Delighted customers are much more likely to become brand advocates. They are so happy with your service they 'tell others'. They will post reviews on your page, engage with your posts and endorse you wherever they can.

So focus on selling benefits not features. This hair salon sells happiness, confidence, feeling good, feeling respected ... not just a wash, cut and blow-dry.

3.3 THE CONTENT FUNNEL

In the last chapter we looked at creating a profile of your ideal customer but realised that not everyone who fits this profile is ready to do business with you. We considered cold, warm and hot audiences and looked at the five stages of customer loyalty: disinterested, suspects, prospects, customers and advocates.

A content funnel helps businesses create content that will appeal to customers as they move through your sales funnel (see section 2.5). (Fig. 3.4)

3.3.1 AWARENESS CONTENT

The top, widest part of the funnel is for awareness or social content. Use this content to introduce new prospects to your page and warm up existing page likes. Awareness content tends to be more social. Remember, people use Facebook as a social network to connect with friends, family and brands. We should also remember that people do business with other people.

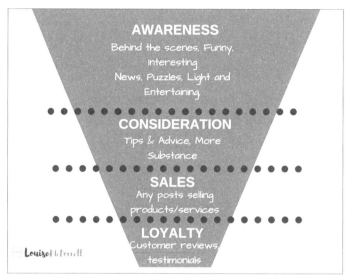

Fig. 3.4

This type of content enables your customers to connect with you and your employees. Your customers get to know you and your staff when they call into your place of business, phone your office, meet you at events and see your photos on your website. Why not use your social media channels to let your customers connect with the people in your organisation? Remember that on Facebook it's good to be social.

For prospects that are cold it gets your brand in front of them. You still need to do a lot of work to warm them up so they consider doing business with you. For existing customers who have not done business with you in some time, it serves as a reminder. For current customers it can be used to reinforce your brand values.

With your employees' permission you could create posts:

Connecting with You and Your Employees

- People joining your organisation
- Staff retiring
- Staff anniversaries

- Engagements and weddings
- Births
- Personal achievements
- Staff achievements
- Achievements of family of staff.

The post on the following page is a great example of this. It was published by Marie Costello on the Savoury Fare Facebook page when one of her staff members, Lorraine Kelly, was celebrating 20 years working at the restaurant. According to Marie, Lorraine is the heart and soul of the restaurant. The post was published on a Friday afternoon and performed extremely well with fans of the page liking, sharing and commenting with their shared memories. The organic reach of the post exceeded 20,000 people, four times the number of people who like the Savoury Fare page. This shows that social media needs to be about people because people connect with other people. The business benefited from increased brand awareness, having their customers comment positively about a staff member and being thought of as a caring employer. (Fig. 3.5)

Behind the Scenes

- Images, video of you and your staff attending a trade or consumer show, a day at the races, etc.
- Sneak previews of refurbishments
- Milestones for the business
- Business awards.

I love this fun post on the following page! A business that specialises in mindfulness celebrated five years in business with a trip to the beach! Engagement levels were high on this post as Facebook fans wanted to show their support to this company and to see more images. (Fig. 3.6)

Fig. 3.5

Fig 3.6

Memes or Inspirational Quotes

Memes, funny and heartwarming pictures, are also a great way to connect with people on social media. Remember that you don't need to 'sell' in every post but just keep your organisation in people's minds. You'll find engagement levels are much higher for this type of post – which means more people in general will see them.

Here is a meme that was published on the Mindfulness Matters Facebook page. I love the way they integrated their website address into the image, so that every time the meme is shared they gain more exposure for their business. (Fig. 3.7)

Fig. 3.7

3.3.2 CONSIDERATION POSTS

As you move prospects along the funnel use consideration or expert content to show how you solve their problems and meet their needs. This is the type of content that will warm prospects to your brand. Use your customer personas to generate content ideas that are all about the customer.

In the previous chapter we discussed the importance of understanding your customers through brainstorming sessions, customer chats and customer surveys. The aim was to identify topics where you have specialist knowledge that your customers may find useful.

For example, a hair stylist can advise on:
- Types of shampoo for different hair types
- How to deal with hair loss
- How to treat itchy scalp.

Or a butcher might answer customers' queries in relation to:
- Hot to cook a Sunday roast
- Recipes for Irish stew
- What to cook for a dinner party.

Or restaurants and gastro pubs can:
- Show how they cater for different dietary requirements
- Advise on wine or craft beer pairings
- Demonstrate how to cook signature dishes.

Think about the questions you get asked continually by your customers. What specialist knowledge do you have that they will be interested in?

You need to make a list of topics and use this as content for your Facebook page. It's important that you post about one topic at a time. One of the most common mistakes business owners make is that they try to include too much advice in one post. Remember that your customers are scrolling down their news feed at speed. To get their attention your post must not only be useful to them, it must also be obvious to them at a glance what it's about. You should try to grab their attention with the first five words. Stop them as they scroll ...

Below are a few posts that work very well. (Fig. 3.8)

Fig. 3.8

This is a post from Sanctum Therapies, a business located outside Ballina in County Mayo. Sanctum Therapies specialises in reflexology for fertility, pregnancy, babies and general well-being. In this video the business owner, Niamh Ryan, demonstrates how to carry out reflexology on a baby to relieve teething pain. This is an example of how you can solve a problem for customers. By helping parents/caretakers relieve teething pain for their babies,

Niamh is building trust in her brand. People are likely to tag or share this post with their friends (with teething babies) because Niamh is offering free, useful advice. This new business had under 600 page likes at the time the post was published, however it had an organic reach of 13,000 and just under 7,000 views.

In this next post Samantha Richardson from Limerick-based Cookie and Crumb is offering timely advice to her fans. She produced a one minute video on how to make pancakes and published it on her page the day before Pancake Tuesday. She also tagged pages in the post that had the potential to share it with their fans. This video was viewed over 5,000 times and the post reached over 15,000 people. Very impressive when you consider that Samantha had 500 page likes at the time. (Fig. 3.9)

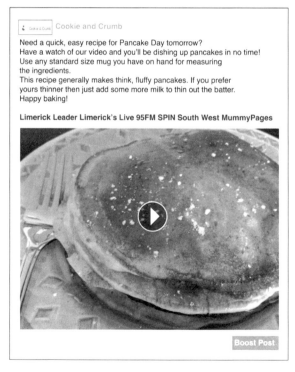

Fig. 3.9

Here is a link to a blog article I wrote some time ago. This is an example of 'evergreen content' as the article, as long as it's relevant and accurate, can be shared on a Facebook page and across other social media channels time and time again. (Fig. 3.10)

Fig. 3.10

3.3.3 NEWS AND INDUSTRY UPDATES

Can you be the first to 'break news' in your industry to your fans? Use information that you pick up at industry events, in periodicals or on industry-related social media channels and blogs to keep your fans in the know. You don't have to the first in the world to break the news – as long as it's news to your fans. It further emphasises your position as an industry expert and helps build trust.

Here is an example of a post that I published on my Facebook group. As soon as I noticed changes on Facebook – in this example, a new way to create audiences for Facebook Ads – I published a post on my group. This is a great way of warming up cold prospects! (Fig. 3.11)

Fig. 3.11

3.3.4 SALES CONTENT

Prospects that are warm to your brand will be most open to sales content. Think carefully about when to publish sales posts on your page and how to target them.

As noted, it's important that your Facebook isn't just full of sales posts. If it is there is a high likelihood that the organic reach (the number of people who see your posts without you having to pay) will be low.

However when producing sales content it's vital you sell the benefits of your products/services. Clearly outline what you are selling and what the prospect should do next if they are interested in buying the product.

I really like this post from Flaunt Ballina for a number of reasons. First of all there are a number of images in the post, so anyone who wants to see all the images needs to click on them. Straight away the page has achieved the engagement of a 'click'. I like the fact that the page owner includes a 'call to action'. The tone of the post is friendly and helpful. All in all it's a great post and it achieved great engagement with 94 reactions, comments and shares, 4,691 post clicks and a reach of 5,960. (Fig. 3.12)

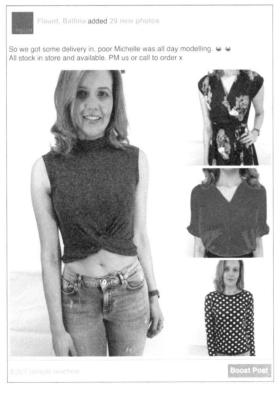

Fig. 3.12

3.3.5 RUNNING COMPETITIONS ON FACEBOOK

Many businesses run competitions on their Facebook pages as a way of growing their likes.

I'm not a big fan of competitions as there is a tendency to attract 'serial competition enterers' as page likes. If these people only like your page to be in with the chance to win a contest, it's unlikely they have any real interest in doing business with you. They are also less likely to engage with your posts which may affect the statistical performance of your page.

However, if you offer a prize that appeals to your target audience and you attract people who are real business prospects, then running a competition is something to consider.

Facebook has clear guidelines around how competitions should be run on business pages. Breaching these guidelines puts your page at risk of being penalised or shut down. Although, with so many 'like and share' competitions doing the rounds it seems there is little enforcement of these terms. I recommend being careful, however, because if Facebook was to start enforcing content rules you may run into problems.

Here are the official Facebook competition terms:

1. Facebook states if you run a competition on your page you are responsible for the lawful operation of that promotion, including:

    -   The official completion rules

    -   The terms and eligibility requirements (for example, age and residency restrictions

    -   Compliance with applicable rules and regulations governing the promotion and all prizes offered (for example, registration and obtaining necessary regulatory approvals).

2. Promotions on Facebook must include the following:

- A complete release of Facebook by each entrant or participant. This means that Facebook holds no responsibility for the competition to anyone who participates.

- Acknowledgement that the promotion is in no way sponsored, endorsed or administered by, or associated with, Facebook.

3. Promotions may be administered on pages or within apps on Facebook. Personal timelines and friend connections must not be used to administer promotions (for example, 'share on your timeline to enter' or 'share on your friend's timeline to get additional entries', and 'tag your friends in this post to enter' are not permitted).

4. Facebook will not assist in the administration of your promotion, and you agree that if you use its service to administer your promotion, you do so at your own risk.

If you run a competition on your page you should include a statement like:

> *By entering this contest, you agree to a complete release of Facebook from any or all liability in connection with this contest. Facebook in no way sponsors, endorses, administers or is associated with this contest.*

You can encourage people to like the competition post and comment on it but you should not ask fans to share the post or tag friends.

For the most up to date content terms see: www.facebook.com/page_guidelines.php.

3.3.6 ADVOCATE CONTENT

Brand advocates are customers who are so satisfied with your business that they tell others about you. In the real world they make recommendations to friends and family. Online, they post reviews on your Facebook page and share your social media posts.

According to a report by McKinsey and Company, word-of-mouth is the biggest factor behind up to 50 per cent of all buying decisions. It has the greatest influence with expensive purchases, or first time purchases, where more research is often required.

Others are much more likely to believe what customers say about you rather than claims you make about your own products and services. For this reason, user-generated content is extremely powerful and worth capturing on your Facebook page in the form of Facebook reviews. (Fig. 3.13)

Fig. 3.13

When customers give you positive feedback, ask them to post a review on your page. Any employees who interact with customers should also be encouraged to ask happy customers for reviews. Similarly, if customers email you with positive feedback, ask them to post it on your page as a review.

If a customer sends you a thank you card, take a photo of it and post it. You don't have to reveal the identity of the sender.

When a customer takes the time to post reviews, take the time to thank them. Consider even taking a screen shot of the review and sharing this as an image on your Facebook page and across other social media channels.

3.4 DEVELOPING A CONTENT CALENDAR

A content calendar is a timetable that details what content is published and when. Content calendars keep you focused and can save time and money. It's also a very useful tool if there is more than one person updating your Facebook page. When everyone on the team knows the content schedule it's easier to delegate tasks to team members.

Content calendars keep your fans and audience interested by preventing your content from stagnating or becoming repetitive. By planning in advance you will be better prepared for key dates. If you wake on April 1st and decide you want to write something funny on your Facebook page for April Fools Day, you have more than likely missed the boat! Content calendars help prevent this.

Here are the steps to follow to develop a content calendar:

1. Consult your goals. What SMART goals have you set for your page? What type of content will you need to publish to achieve them? For example, if your goal is to increase traffic to your website from your Facebook page, then you need to publish posts that link to it.

2. Come up with content for your page that fits your customer personas (see section 3.2).

3. Tune into how each post is performing on your page. Underneath each post you can see how many people the post reached (was viewed by). See what kind of content is resonating with your audience. If they like memes, publish more of them. Don't publish humorous posts if the reach on these posts is low.

4. Write down key dates for your business, employees, sector and wider industry. Remember to include bank holidays, changes in legislation and to tune into trends locally and internationally.

5. Consider a theme-based weekly post, like #Throwback-Tuesday or #MotivationMonday.

6. Use an electronic calendar to create a content schedule planning content that is not time-specific in advance. Remember, however, that it is important to leave some scope to react in real time to news and any other changes in your business or sector.

3.5 HOW TO UPDATE YOUR FACEBOOK PAGE

If you are using a laptop or PC to update your Facebook page you will have the option to:

- Share a photo or video
- Advertise your business
- Write a note
- Get messages
- Get phone calls
- Create an event
- Create an offer
- Help people find your business.

The options you have available will depend on what type of page you have, the category you have selected and what template you have selected for your page. (Fig. 3.14)

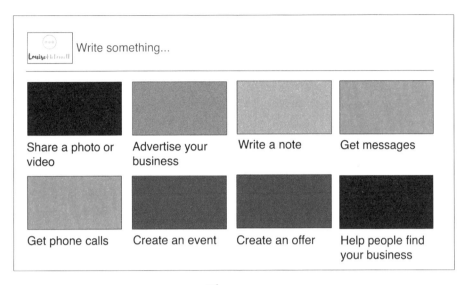

Fig. 3.14

3.5.1 SHARE A PHOTO OR VIDEO

Select the option 'share a photo or video' to upload a photo or a video from your computer (Fig. 3.15). The image or video must first be saved on your computer to do this. Remember where you have saved the image or video. You can even create a 'Facebook' folder on your computer.

You will be presented with the option to:

- Upload photos/video (you can upload up to five images here or a video to your status). If I am creating or resizing images to upload to Facebook I use 1200 pixels x 900 pixels.

- Create a photo album. These images tend to be square – I generally use 600 x 600 pixels. When you're uploading an album, bear in mind that you can publish it as a post on your page but for the moment you can't schedule this type of post.

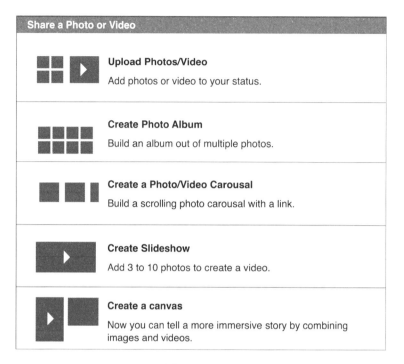

Fig. 3.15

- Create a Photo/Video Carousel. Use this option if you want to link your images to a website. You will be prompted to insert a destination URL (address for a specific website) for the images. Facebook will find any images from the URL. You can choose whether you want to use these images by selecting or unselecting them. You can select up to five square images. I recommend using 600 x 600 pixels. You can add a 100 character description with each image and a separate destination URL (link to a website page).

- Create a Canvas. This is displayed on mobile phones only and uses a combination of full screen images and video to give an impressive display about your brand. The recommended size for images is 1200 x 628 pixels. Images may not include more than 20 per cent text.

3.5.2 TIPS FOR USING IMAGES ON FACEBOOK

1. Use images or videos whenever possible. Posts with images will receive up to 179 per cent more notice in the news feed. Remember that people are flicking down through their news feed at speed. You need to catch their attention as they scroll. Using a good image can achieve this. Sometimes you may need to think outside the box to come up with a relevant image but it's worth it. The more your image stands out in the news feed, the more successful your post with be.

2. Using good images also increases the likelihood of people clicking on the post. This counts as a post engagement which should have a positive impact on the number of people that see the post in general as well as future posts.

3. Ensure you have permission to use the images. People ask if it's okay to take images from Google to use on their Facebook pages? No, you must get permission to use images under copyright. Use sites like Pexels.com, Pixabay.com or Unsplash.com to get free or nearly free stock photos.

4. When resizing images keep the proportions so they won't look skewed. Don't use images that are low quality as they will appear blurry. Use tools like Canva.com, Pic Monkey or Photoshop to resize images.

5. Where possible integrate your logo and brand colours. This reinforces your brand identity and helps customers to connect with you.

6. Use less than 20 per cent text on your images as they generally perform better in the news feed and as boosted posts.

3.5.3 ADVERTISE YOUR BUSINESS

For detailed information on Facebook Ads – see section 5.

3.5.4 WRITE A NOTE

Facebook notes have been around for a long time, but recently have had a facelift and are beginning to look more like a blog article. This is great news for bloggers and small business owners. There is an image at the top with text below which can be formatted to include headings, subheadings, bullet points and other ways of highlighting text.

It's also possible to include a 'note' tab on the left hand side of your page where people can find a list of all your notes.

The recommended image dimensions for a note are 1200 x 445 pixels. If you upload a smaller image, it will stretch to this size and appear blurry.

3.5.5 REQUEST A MESSAGE

This will create a post on your Facebook page using your cover photo as the post image. You can change the image by clicking on it and uploading a different one from your computer. It's also possible to edit the text below the image by clicking it. The 'call to action' (what you want the reader to do next) for the post is 'send message'. You also have the opportunity to write something at the top of the post to compel more people to send a message to you.

3.5.6 REQUEST A PHONE CALL

This will create a post on your page in the very same way as the 'get messages' option, but the call to action in this case will be to get people to phone you.

3.5.7 HELP PEOPLE FIND YOUR BUSINESS

This will create a post in the same way as 'get messages', but in this case it will give people directions to find your business.

3.5.8 CREATE AN EVENT

See section 1.12.

3.6 OTHER WAYS TO UPDATE YOUR PAGE

3.6.1 POSTING A VIDEO FROM YOUTUBE

To share a video from YouTube, you need to navigate to the video on YouTube. Click on 'share' which is located under the video title. (Fig. 3.16)

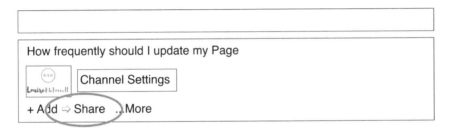

Fig. 3.16

When you select 'share' you will see the following. (Fig. 3.17)

Fig. 3.17

Highlight the ULR in the box and copy the link. Then navigate back to your Facebook page and paste the link into your text panel. (Fig. 3.18)

Fig. 3.18

Remember to tell your audience why they should watch the video. Don't assume that they will know what it's about. Think carefully about what you can say about the video that will compel them to watch it.

3.6.2 POSTING A LINK TO A WEBSITE OR BLOG ARTICLE

To share a page from your website or an article you have found on someone else's website navigate to the page/article you wish to share. Highlight the ULR from the address bar, right click and select 'copy'. (Fig. 3.19)

Fig. 3.19

Then navigate to the Facebook page on which you wish to share the link. Right click on your mouse and select paste. (Fig. 3.20)

Remember to include a good description to let your audience know why they should read the article.

Fig. 3.20

If the page you are sharing has an image it may appear. If you want to use another image, unselect the image and press the + to upload another one (Fig. 3.21)

Fig. 3.21

3.6.3 SHARING A POST FROM ANOTHER PAGE ON YOUR PAGE

If you find a post on another Facebook page you wish to share, simply select 'share' underneath the post. (Fig. 3.22)

Fig. 3.22

Next click on the option at the top of the screen that pops up. Select 'share on a page you manage'. (Fig. 3.23)

Fig. 3.23

Explain why are you sharing this post. Try to minimise the number of posts from other pages that you share. The organic reach of posts that are shared from other pages is generally lower than if you create an original post. If you want to help another business or organisation by sharing their article, video or event consider using the same image they have used, giving the same detail and tagging the business rather than sharing the post.

3.6.4 Driving Traffic to Your Blog from Facebook

Having a blog on your website can improve how your website performs in Google. Google loves fresh content, packed full of keyword phrases that are relevant to your business. Once you have published new articles you will want to send as much traffic to them as possible. Links to the article from your social media channels not only achieve this but also assist with search engine optimisation (SEO). When Google sees lots of links from other websites back to your blog, it knows the content on your blog must be good. Links from social media posts count in this regard, as does 'social attribution', the popularity of the social media post which is determined by the number of people engaging with that post (clicking, reacting, commenting, sharing).

Facebook is one of the top platforms for driving traffic to your blog. Your challenge when publishing a link to a new blog article is to get people to click through to read it. The ultimate goal is to get people to react, comment or share the article as well as click on it.

When you are sharing a link to your new blog article there are a number of things you need to get right. You will need a good image, a link to the article (copy and paste the URL in the address bar) and some reason to encourage your fans to click through. What can you say in your post that will make people want to read your article? Can you intrigue them in some way? Don't try to do this if you're in a hurry – you need time to be creative! Aim to catch your fans' attention in the first five words!

When sharing an article from your blog copy the URL from the address bar rather than using the 'social share' buttons from the article. (Fig. 3.24)

Fig. 3.24

When you share using the Facebook Icon, depending on the website functionality, you have less control over how your post looks. You may not be able to change the image. (Fig. 3.25)

Fig. 3.25

In the image on the following page, I am sharing the same article. In Fig. 3.26 I have shared the article using the Facebook icon embedded on the website, and in Fig. 3.27 I have copied and pasted the article URL into the status update. This method gives me more flexibility. I can unselect the image and choose a different one if I wish.

Fig. 3.26

Fig. 3.27

3.6.5 SCHEDULING A POST ON YOUR FACEBOOK PAGE

To schedule a post, simply create it as you normally would by writing text, adding images/video etc. and then, instead of pressing publish, click the dropdown menu to the right and select 'schedule'. (Fig. 3.28)

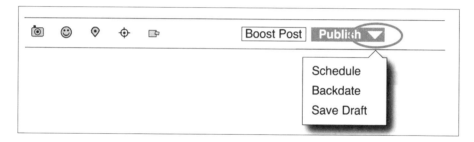

Fig. 3.28

Select the time and the date you wish the post to be published. This is a very useful feature for the following reasons:

- You can prepare posts at a time that suits you and publish when you know your audience is likely to engage with them.

- You can organise your working week by preparing multiple posts at the one time.

- You can prepare posts in advance of an event.

- You can preview what a post will look like before it is published by reviewing it under publishing tools at the top of your page.

3.7 UPDATING YOUR PAGE USING A SMART PHONE

Using your smart phone is a great way of updating your page on the go. Keep your fans up to date with new products, new stock, events you are attending! Hairstylists, builders, interior designers, and makeup artists can use their phones to take before and after photos or videos. Fashion boutiques, garden centres, furniture stores, gift shops and jewellers can easily catalogue new stock as it arrives in. Tour guides, dog walkers, photographers, wood turners, archaeologists and food producers can capture the changing landscape as they go about their work.

Images or video taken on your phone can be uploaded to your Facebook page instantly. All you need is a steady hand, internet access and the Facebook or Pages Manager App.

Posts can be published immediately from your phone or scheduled to go out at a later date. It's also possible to edit scheduled posts from a laptop. I find this useful when I want to add meaningful descriptions with links and tags to each image.

Use your smart phone to record videos and broadcast live from your Facebook page. Live broadcasts appear higher in the news feed when they are live and as a video on your page when they are no longer live. Facebook notifies your fans that you are live to build the audience while you are broadcasting. For more on Facebook Live see section 4.4.4.

While I recommend using your phone on the go, there is more functionality and administrative options available on a desktop for managing and updating Facebook pages as well as using Facebook ads.

3.8 SIX WAYS OF REPRESENTING YOUR BRAND ON FACEBOOK

Creating a visual identity for your business is one of the most fundamental elements of your marketing strategy. Often businesses spend time and money developing multiple marketing materials that bear no resemblance to each other. One company has printed business cards, another has printed brochures, a local sign company has produced road signs, a specialist embroidery company has created t-shirts and hoodies – and they all look different. Different colours, fonts and even variations on the company name are common mistakes.

Once when traveling to Mexico my twins, Jack and Ruth, then pre-schoolers, were impressed with the Virgin Atlantic airplane and wanted their photograph taken with the plane in the background. A few months later we were travelling in the UK when a Virgin Atlantic train swished past and my daughter piped up, 'Look Mammy, there's the Mexico plane'.

For me that's what branding is all about. If someone sees your road sign, then later a business card, brochure, t-shirt or the sign over your business door will they know it's the same business? And will they make the connection between your printed material and your website or Facebook page?

If you don't have a business logo, engage the services of a graphic designer and get one developed. Shop around and find a graphic designer that best meets your budget. When you have a logo developed get the colour references from your graphic designer and ensure that all printers, web developers and graphic designers use these colours consistently. Also get recommendations from your designer in terms of what fonts to use for print and online. When developing your logo, your graphic designer may charge an additional fee to create a Brand Guidelines document. This is a style guide to anyone using your logo. If you cannot afford to have this document developed, at the very least establish the fonts and brand colours. You can then use these references yourself when creating your own images in Canva, Photoshop, etc.

3.8.1 PROFILE PICTURE

The profile picture holds one of the most dominating positions on your Facebook page. Companies and brands should use their logo as the profile picture. If your logo is rectangular you can get a square or stacked version created for use on social media.

Sole traders should consider using a professional photograph of themselves for their profile picture, integrating the brand subtly if possible, either on your clothing or in the background.

Your profile picture is also used as the thumbnail for your page, so check that it works well at that size.

3.8.2 COVER PICTURE

Use an image or video that represents your brand and communicates your value proposition. Your cover picture can change to place greater emphasis on events, milestones and the seasonality of your business.

According to Facebook, the recommended file is a JPG file that's 820 pixels wide, 312 pixels tall and less than 100 kilobytes. It's also recommended that there is:

- No contact information

- No 'calls to action' (book now, call here to order)

- No arrows pointing to the 'like' button.

The recommended size for video covers is 820 x 462 pixels, however it is required that videos be at least 820 x 312 pixels.

Once you have published a cover image, it will appear as a post on your page. You can click on the image or video and add a description which will appear with the post. That description will always appear alongside that image, so keep it generic if you plan using the image again in the future.

3.8.3 IMAGES POSTS

When creating images for your page it's important to integrate brand colours and fonts and where possible your logo. This makes your page look professional and keeps your brand top of mind with fans. Use image editing tools like Canva, Pic Monkey, Photoshop, Microsoft Paint to create images in line with your brand guidelines.

3.8.4 VIDEOS

As the appetite for video content grows on Facebook, you need to think of new ways to produce quality videos on your page. Where possible, consider how you can integrate your logo into the video. Can you use a branded pull up stand or perhaps some shop signage in the background? Do you have branded clothes or a uniform you can use? Or can you use video editing software to integrate your logo as a watermark on your video?

3.8.5 BRAND STORY

What is your brand story? What is your promise to customers? Have you integrated this into your page setup? Remember that if a competitor can take the description from your page and copy and paste it into theirs, it's not good enough. Write a short and long description that is completely unique to your company. Remember to integrate why your customers 'like' you. What makes them choose you over your competitors?

3.8.6 BRAND VOICE

When you are creating posts on your Facebook page it's important to keep your brand voice consistent. How do you speak to customers in the real world? Remember that Facebook is a social network so remember to be social. Don't treat Facebook as a place where you spam your fans with ads. Keep your customer personas in mind (see section 2.2) and when you are writing your posts imagine that you are speaking directly to them.

If you're starting out and are nervous about posting on your page, you might place a picture of your ideal customer on your desk and think about what you would say to them in the real world. Don't be afraid of not getting it perfect right away – just start posting and over time you will find your voice.

Chapter 4

MAXIMISING ORGANIC REACH ON FACEBOOK

There is a common misconception that you must be advertising on Facebook in order to achieve good reach, meaning the number of people or fans who actually see your posts. *The organic reach of a page refers to the number of people who see your posts without you having to pay for it.*

The organic reach of your page depends on a number of factors, such as the number of likes or followers your page has. The more likes or fans a page has the more people are likely to see the posts published. The engagement levels that you currently have on your page also contribute to the organic reach of your posts.

So what is considered an engagement? If someone likes, comments, shares or clicks on a post this is considered an engagement. People seem more likely to click on a post to 'see more' if some of the text of a post is hidden. They might not like, comment or share the post but will still click the 'see more' to read the entire post. This type of engagement is also tracked by Facebook and is often the easiest way to get people to engage.

The higher the engagement levels on your page, the more Facebook will show your posts in the news feeds of your fans. If your posts are boring, repetitive and of poor quality, and if over time the engagement levels are consistently poor, so too will be the organic reach of your page.

So how do you maximise your chances of achieving higher engagement levels and thus a better organic reach?

4.1 USE MEDIA-RICH CONTENT WITH EVERY POST

Always use an image or a video with every post. Text-only posts simply get much less notice in the news feed. Adding an image or a video to your post will increase its organic reach by between 50 per cent and 180 per cent. Even when you think your post doesn't merit an image, think outside the box and find one that is suitable. The better the image the more attention it will attract in the news feed.

The image serves three main purposes: to get the attention of people in the news feed (stop them as they scroll), to communicate the subject of the post and to raise brand awareness. (Fig. 4.1)

Fig. 4.1

Remember that people are generally scrolling on their phones so you need an image to help your post to stand out. If your fans stop engaging with your posts (liking, commenting, sharing, clicking), it will reduce the general reach of your page. If your fans stop engaging with your posts, Facebook assumes they are not interested in your content in general. That's why it's important to consider every post you publish carefully. If you're in a hurry and don't have time to find an image, don't post at all until you have the time to do it properly.

Fig. 4.2

The image in the above post is simple yet effective. It incorporates my business's logo, uses brand colours, is the correct size and has less than 20 per cent text. Facebook used to apply a text rule whereby images with more than 20 per cent text could not be used in boosted posts and other Facebook Ads. Although Facebook has relaxed this rule, they still advise that images with over 20 per cent text will not reach as many people and may cost more as a result. To check what percentage of your image includes text check the Facebook Grip Tool at https://www.facebook.com/ads/tools/text_overlay.

4.2 USE IMAGES OF THE CORRECT SIZE

Use images of good quality, for which you have copyright and that are the correct size for Facebook, that is, 1200 x 900 pixels. If images are the incorrect size they will appear justified to the left in the desktop news feed. It's less obvious on a smart phone as the screen is smaller. (Fig. 4.3)

Fig. 4.3

In the post above, you can see that the image is too small. It is sitting to the left on the screen.

Many small businesses tend to publish posters on their pages. I recommend against this generally as posters will be the incorrect size and will have too much text. When an image has over 20 per cent text it may not be approved for a 'boost post' (when you pay Facebook to show your post to more people) and even if it is approved you may find that your ad is expensive. Instead, take one of the images from the poster, resize it to the recommended size and use the poster content as the image description. Type your description where it says, 'Say something about this photo'.

Here is an example of a post with a strong visual. The image is the correct size so it looks more professional. It integrates my company logo and uses brand colours. There is some text on the image to draw attention to the subject of the post. (Fig. 4.4)

Fig. 4.4

4.3 USE IMAGE DESCRIPTIONS

Posting images without descriptions is one of the most common mistakes businesses make. This is like holding up an image in front of someone but not telling them what it is about or why you are showing it to them. You need to tell your audience what it is you are sharing, why you are sharing it and why you believe it is of interest to them. Don't assume your audience will know why you're sharing the image ... remember, they are scrolling. Even if you are sharing a link to a website article or video and there is a snippet of the article underneath the image, you still need to tell your audience why you are sharing it with them.

One post that stands out in my memory is one of a car appearing to drive out of a hotel's banqueting room wall! It just looked so unusual and there was plenty of scope for the hotel to have had fun with the post. They could have come up with a funny comment or even asked their fans to come up with a caption for the image. The image was in fact a candy cart! But without a description the post got no engagement and was a missed opportunity.

Use an image editing tool to resize images to the correct size. You should also integrate your logo where possible, your brand colours and fonts as well.

I am a big fan of Canva, an online graphic design website. It's easy to use and has a free version which has excellent functionality. It has saved templates of popular design types including marketing material, email marketing headers and social media channels. In relation to Facebook it has templates for cover images, event cover images and Facebook post. It's also possible to create images using custom dimensions.

4.4 USE VIDEO

I find that many small business owners think that video is beyond them, that it's just for larger companies with big budgets. Not so! Every business should be considering how it can integrate video into its marketing communications strategy. Thanks to smart phones, recording video has never been so available or easy. Smart phones are packed with powerful functions to enable you to record HD videos any time, any place.

One of the main reasons why you should consider video is because consumers love it. Video posts are even better than posts with images! According to a study by the marketing company

Socialbakers, the organic reach of a video post is 135 per cent greater than a photo post.

According to Cisco, traffic from online videos will constitute over 80 per cent of all consumer internet traffic by 2020. YouTube reports that video consumption rates are rising 100 per cent every year. And according to a study by Defy Media, teens and young adults watch more videos per week on YouTube than TV.

Since 2015 there has been an explosion in the use of video on Facebook. Facebook users increased the number of videos posted per person by 75 per cent globally in 2015. That year there were 8 billion video views per day which represented a 100 per cent growth in six months.

In 2015 Facebook commissioned Nielsen to analyse data on how video ads affect brand metrics. The three metrics they considered as part of the study were: ad recall, brand awareness and purchase consideration.

The results of the study revealed that even people who did not watch the video saw the ad featuring the video. As expected, the impact of the video increased the longer people watched it. One of the most interesting statistics I took from the survey was that even video views of 10 seconds effectively build awareness and drive purchase intent.

4.4.1 NATIVE VIDEO

Videos that are uploaded directly to Facebook are called native videos. (Fig. 4.6)

To upload a native video, go to your page. Select 'photo/video' as shown in the image above. Then select a video from your computer/laptop. Similarly you can upload a video from your smart phone. (Fig. 4.7)

Fig. 4.6

← Posting as Louise McDonnell

Louise McDonnell
Public

What's on your mind?

Photo/Video

Go Live

Check in

Feeling/Activity

Tag product

Fig. 4.7

Using the Pages Manager Facebook app select 'photo/video' as shown in the image above. Then select a video from your gallery.

When uploading native videos remember to integrate relevant keyword phrases in the video title and description. This will assist the video being indexed for relevant searches.

The benefits of uploading native videos directly to Faceook are:

- Videos autoplay.
- A video is considered to be viewed at three seconds.
- Adding captions to videos increases the watch time by 12 per cent, on average.
- 74 per cent of total ad recall is achieved in 10 seconds of Facebook video campaigns.
- There are in-depth statistics for videos available in Facebook Insights on:
  ◇ Number of minutes watched
  ◇ Video views
  ◇ 10 second views
  ◇ Unique viewers
  ◇ Average time video is watched
  ◇ Audience and engagement.
- After watching a video, 64 per cent of users are more likely to complete an online purchase.

4.4.2 CREATING VIDEO CONTENT

Create content that will appeal to your customer. As with all social media posts, your content needs to be really good. *Remember that it's not about what you want to say about your products and services, it's about what your customers want to hear from you.* It's not about you, it's about them.

- Aim to draw your viewer in immediately. Begin your video with the most important content. Don't bury it midway through your video as your viewers will more than likely have scrolled on to the next post by then.
- Consider integrating video captions at the beginning of your video to draw in views and communicate the subject of your broadcast.
- Try to draw your viewer in within the first 10 words.

- Be as concise as possible. Shorter videos of 20 to 30 seconds have more chances of being watched than longer ones.

- Be authentic and true to your brand and integrate your logo subtly if possible.

- If you're nervous about recording, write a script and then practice it until you're comfortable enough to record it.

- Use your phone to record and re-record until you get it right!

4.4.3 TIPS FOR RECORDING ON YOUR SMART PHONE

- Avoid zooming as this can impact on the quality of your video.

- Record your video in good natural light or in a room with good lighting. Otherwise your video may appear dark.

- Avoid recording in a room that is empty or where there might be an echo.

- Record in high definition if possible. Check the video settings on your phone to select this option. Facebook recommends the following settings:

  - ◇ H.264 video with AAC audio in MOV or MP4 format

  - ◇ An aspect ratio no larger than 1280 pixels wide and divisible by 16 pixels

  - ◇ A frame rate at, or below, 30fps

  - ◇ Stereo audio with a sample rate of 44,100hz.

4.4.4 FACEBOOK LIVE

Facebook Live enables you to broadcast live from your Facebook page to fans all over the world. To 'go live' navigate to your page using your smart phone. Select the 'go live' option as shown in the image on the following page. (Fig. 4.8)

Fig. 4.8

When broadcasting live ensure you have a strong internet connection. Then set a date and a time to go live. People will tune in if they find your broadcasts newsworthy, useful, educational, funny or inspirational.

Once you have set a time and a date for going live, remember to tell your fans. You can post on your Facebook page, boost that post, email or text them. Try to build excitement about your live broadcast; give your audience a reason to tune in.

Write a compelling description before going live as this will appear in the news feed alongside your video. It's a good idea to have this typed out in advance so you can paste it into the description dialogue box just before you go live. You can also edit the description after the video is no longer live.

Once live, you will see the number of people who are watching. There is always a slight delay on the page so your fans will be a few seconds behind you. You'll see fans' comments as they publish them. It's a good idea to mention fans that have commented and answer any questions if you can as this encourages others to interact. After your live broadcast it is recommended to respond to all comments.

Facebook Live videos are more likely to appear higher in the news feed when those videos are actually live, as compared to when they are no longer live. It is estimated that people spend three times longer watching live video compared to videos that are no longer live.

Before broadcasting live on your page you should test it on your own profile. You can choose the visibility setting 'only me'. In this way you can run multiple tests which will only be visible to you.

If you are planning to record the broadcast on your phone, test how it looks both in landscape and portrait. Some android phones display live video recorded on landscape sideways in the Facebook desktop news feed. Test in advance and if this is the case with your phone stick to portrait.

Be sure you have permission to record in the location and that you have cleared copyright for any music used. If Facebook suspects a copyright infringement, especially for music, it will remove your live video.

The sound quality of your broadcast is important. If more than one person is involved in the broadcast consider using an external microphone that connects with your phone or computer.

Choose a location with good natural light or use a well-lit location. A tripod is useful because not only is it portable, but you can raise and lower it to the optimum height.

Currently you need to use third party apps like BlueJeans or BeLive.tv if you wish to broadcast using a computer. These apps give a professional touch to live broadcasts as guests can join the broadcast remotely and images can be shared from the host's computer.

4.4.5 SLIDESHOWS

Slideshows are a great way of creating a video using images either on their own or with a soundtrack. Slideshows can include images from different events or historical images in a video. If you have a recording of a radio ad you have previously used on local or national radio you can use this as the soundtrack for your slide-show. Apps like InShot, Slideshow Maker and Picasso are free, easy to use and can produce high quality slideshows in minutes.

4.4.6 UPLOADING LINKS TO VIDEOS ON OTHER CHANNELS

To share videos from other social media channels like YouTube or Vimeo, copy and paste a link to the video in the status panel as shown in the image below. Remember to write a description that will encourage viewers to watch your video. (Fig. 4.9)

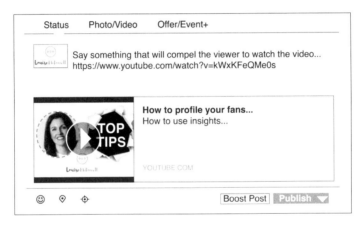

Fig. 4.9

4.4.7 TIPS FOR MANAGING VIDEOS ON YOUR PAGE

- Once you upload a video to your page, click on the icon on the bottom right hand corner of the screen as seen below. Select the option 'HD'. This will play your video in high definition if it has been recorded that way. Select 'more settings' to bring you to a section where you can adjust settings to play all videos in HD. (Fig. 4.10)

- Under the video section on your page you can set a 'featured video'. Featured videos are prominently displayed on your page, especially on smartphones.

Fig. 4.10

- You can also create playlists. Give each play list a title and description and remember to integrate key words.

- Crossposting is a way to share videos across multiple pages. Crossposting can only happen between pages that have added each other. You control which videos you want to crosspost. When a page crossposts your videos, it will also be able to view video insights for its posts.

4.5 TAG OTHER PAGES

The success of a Facebook business page depends on the ability to consistently create good quality posts that perform well in the news feed. Facebook is a social network and tagging is a great way to reach out to relevant pages that may in turn share your posts, thus improving organic reach for your page.

4.5.1 WHAT IS TAGGING?

When you tag a business page on Facebook, it creates a link to that page. Admins also receive a notification advising them that their page has been 'mentioned'. This will be visible as a 'notification' and will also appear in the 'activity log' under 'mentions'.

The post with the tag won't go into the news feed of the business you have tagged unless they share it with their fans.

4.5.2 RECOMMENDATIONS WHEN TAGGING OTHER BUSINESS PAGES

- Don't be afraid to tag. The worst thing that can happen is that your tag isn't acknowledged or shared. No big deal.

- Tag business pages that you have mentioned in your post. It's a great way to let them know that you are talking about them. Social networking is all about having conversations and tagging is a great mechanism to facilitate this. It may result in your post being shared on the page you have tagged or the page admin may create a new post mentioning (and tagging) your page. All good!

- Tag businesses you wish to thank, acknowledge (sponsors, stakeholders, etc.), form alliances with, and so on. Whenever you create a post give yourself some time to consider which businesses could be tagged.

- Also consider other pages that may be interested in your post and tag them at the end. For example, a business writing about their new product or service may tag the local Chamber of Commerce business page or the local town or county page. A tourism entity may tag their regional or national tourism-related pages and so on. Think outside the box. Consider the pages in your industry that may be looking for interesting content.

- Posts that tend to be shared are generally well crafted with good content and visuals. Only tag pages if the information in your post is good enough to merit sharing. Consider tagging if you've captured an amazing photo, written a blog article with some good advice, created a video with a different angle on a subject, etc.

- Maximise your pages chances of being tagged by other pages by ensuring that the 'tagging ability' is turned on in your page settings.

4.5.3 HOW TO TAG A BUSINESS ON YOUR FAN PAGE

Create a tag by typing '@' immeditaly followed by the page's username (@username). You will find a page's username directly underneath the page name which is located on the right of the profile picture. (Fig. 4.11)

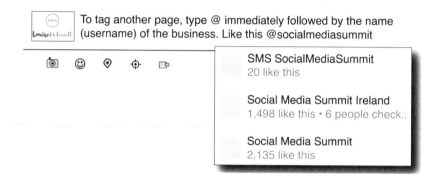

Fig. 4.11

Pick the page you want to tag from the suggestions that appear. The @ symbol will disappear and when your post is published the tagged business will appear in blue. This shows your audience that the blue text is a link to that business's Facebook page.

Sometimes it can be difficult to tag using a smart phone. A good workaround is to schedule the post for a future date and then use your computer to edit the post and create the tag. Scheduled posts are found under 'publishing tools' on the admin panel of your page (see Fig. 4.15 on page 136).

4.6 ENCOURAGE ENGAGEMENT

Write your post in a way that will encourage engagement or intrigue your reader. What can you say in your post that will grab the attention of your fans? The first five to ten words are crucial. What problem are you solving? What news are you imparting?

What's the big deal? Don't fall into the trap of 'warming up' to what you have to say. Don't bury the most interesting information in the third or fourth line – lead with it!

If you're posting a link to a video, what can you say about that video to encourage people to click through? If you're posting some advice to your fans, what problem are you solving? Lead with this!

What you say in your post will have a major impact on what your fans do. Can you include a 'call to action'? Can you ask them to 'click like' if they agree with the sentiment of the post? Can you ask them their opinion about something? Ask them to comment by choosing between different options.

4.7 TIMING IS IMPORTANT

Publish posts when your fans are most likely to be using Facebook. In the insights section of your page, check out the 'posts' tab where you will find another tab, 'when your fans are online'. This shows you the best days and times you should be posting. The graph tells you the days of the week your fans are on and the times of the day. You can see when people are sleeping, when they wake (there is a little spike at 8.00 am), there is steady usage of Facebook throughout the day (people have it on their smart phones) and then the graph increases in the evening. (Fig. 4.12)

The graph tells you when your audience is on (using Facebook), but you need to consider when they are most likely to engage. Remember the Facebook algorithm (see section 1.10): when your fans engage with your posts (react, comment, share, click or watch just three seconds of your videos), Facebook knows they are interested in the content of your page and are more likely to show your posts to these fans in the future.

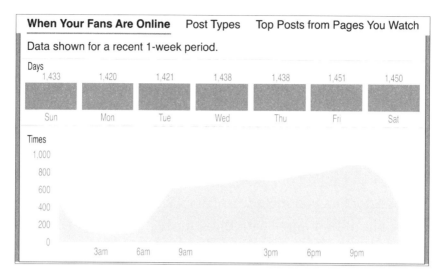

Fig. 4.12

However, the only way you will know the best time to post is through trial and error. Again, consulting Facebook insights will assist you. Look back at posts you have published. Is there a pattern emerging? Are you getting better engagement first thing in the morning? At lunchtime? In the evening? The figure on the following page shows you the day of the week and time (on the left hand side) when posts were published. It also gives a summary of the post, the type (image, video, text, link etc.), the targeting, the reach and engagement. Look at the reach and compare this to the time of day and day of the week that the post was published. Have you published similar posts that performed better on one day or at a particular time of the day? Every page's audience is different. The only way you will learn this is by analysing the results from previous posts. (Fig. 4.13)

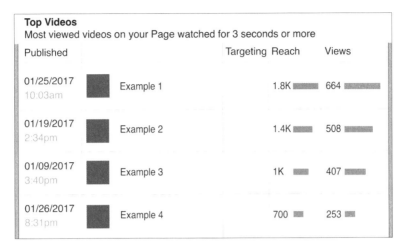

Fig. 4.13

4.8 SCHEDULE POSTS

Use the 'scheduling' option on Facebook to schedule posts. If the optimum time for your fans is 10.00 pm at night, simply schedule your post to publish at this time.

To schedule a post, instead of publishing it click the dropdown menu to the right of 'publish' and select the option to 'schedule'. You can then select the time and date you wish the post to be published. (Fig. 4.14)

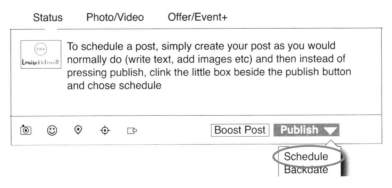

Fig. 4.14

There is no limit on the number of posts you can schedule which is useful if you want to publish a few weeks' worth of posts before you go on holidays or enter a busy time for your business.

Scheduled posts appear under 'publishing tools' which is found on the administrative panel of your page. (Fig. 4.15)

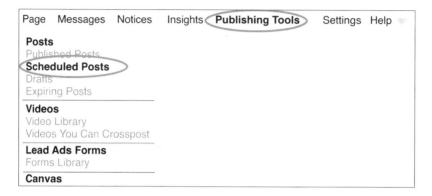

Fig. 4.15

4.9 CREATE ORIGINAL POSTS RATHER THAN ALWAYS SHARING

Although there are times when you will want to help out another business or organisation by sharing a post from their page, I advise against doing this too frequently. Posts shared from other pages rarely achieve good organic reach. Instead of sharing, create a new post on your page. You can upload the same image (once you have permission to use it), tag the page that created the post initially and link it to their website/event etc. This will ensure consistency on your page by maintaining a good organic reach with every post.

4.10 USE HASHTAGS

Although hashtags are more widely used on other social media channels, it is possible to use them on Facebook as well. Hashtags are search terms and can increase the visibility of posts for related searches.

4.11 RATE YOUR LAST FACEBOOK POST

How good was your most recent Facebook post? Use the assessment card on the following page to score it! The techniques outlined in this chapter will help you to achieve a high score. Think of this assessment card every time you create a post. It will help maximise organic reach and make boosted posts (see section 5.5) more successful.

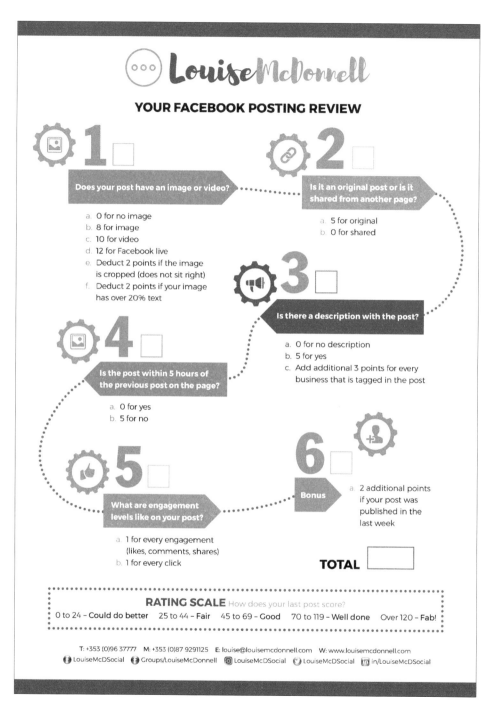

YOUR FACEBOOK POSTING REVIEW

1

Does your post have an image or video?

a. 0 for no image
b. 8 for image
c. 10 for video
d. 12 for Facebook live
e. Deduct 2 points if the image is cropped (does not sit right)
f. Deduct 2 points if your image has over 20% text

2

Is it an original post or is it shared from another page?

a. 5 for original
b. 0 for shared

3

Is there a description with the post?

a. 0 for no description
b. 5 for yes
c. Add additional 3 points for every business that is tagged in the post

4

Is the post within 5 hours of the previous post on the page?

a. 0 for yes
b. 5 for no

5

What are engagement levels like on your post?

a. 1 for every engagement (likes, comments, shares)
b. 1 for every click

6

Bonus

a. 2 additional points if your post was published in the last week

TOTAL

RATING SCALE How does your last post score?
0 to 24 – **Could do better**   25 to 44 – **Fair**   45 to 69 – **Good**   70 to 119 – **Well done**   Over 120 – **Fab!**

T: +353 (0)96 37777   M: +353 (0)87 9291125   E: louise@louisemcdonnell.com   W: www.louisemcdonnell.com
LouiseMcDSocial   Groups/LouiseMcDonnell   LouiseMcDSocial   LouiseMcDSocial   in/LouiseMcDSocial

Fig. 4.16

Chapter 5

INTRODUCTION TO FACEBOOK ADS

Facebook advertising is one of the most powerful marketing tools available to businesses. Facebook ads can reach people on a scale similar to TV.

Facebook ads work! If someone you know says they used them in the past and didn't find them any good perhaps they weren't using them effectively. There are so many factors that contribute to the success rate of ads. Were they targeting the right audience? Did they use good images or video? Did they write compelling ad copy?

There is nothing to compare to Facebook ads in terms of targeting potential customers. When people set up profiles they share information relating to their demographics. Facebook can further profile consumers using information relating to brands and pages they connect with, as well as the content.

Facebook collects hundreds of data points on every user which can be used by advertisers to target their ideal customers. Here are just some examples:

1. Location
2. Age
3. Generation
4. Gender

5. Language

6. Education level

7. Relationship status (unspecified, married, engaged, in a relationship)

8. Sexual orientation

9. Interests and hobbies

10. Type of smart phone used

11. Home ownership and type

12. People with an anniversary within 30 days

13. Parents

14. Expectant parents

15. Mothers, divided by 'type' (soccer, trendy, etc.)

16. People who are likely to engage in politics

17. Job title

18. Office type

19. Interests

20. People who have created a Facebook event

21. People who have used Facebook Payments

22. Administrators of Facebook pages

23. Expats (divided by what country they are from originally)

24. People who belong to a credit union, national bank or regional bank

25. People who tend to shop online (or off)

26. People who travel frequently, for work or pleasure

27. Type of holidays people take

28. People who recently returned from a trip

29. People who recently used a travel app.

Facebook ads enables businesses both large and small to tap into this to reach people who are most likely to become customers.

Anyone who has a Facebook business page can use Facebook ads. This offers small businesses the same opportunity as large multinationals. Businesses set their own budget and spend as much or as little as they wish. If you want to spend €5 per day, once your budget is used up, your ads stop showing.

People don't have to like your page in order to see your ads. In fact, Facebook ads are a great way to reach beyond the people who already like your page. You select what audience you wish to reach. That's why it's so important to have defined your ideal customers in Chapter 2. Later in this chapter I'll be showing you a number of different ways to create audiences for your ads.

You don't need a big budget to get Facebook ads to work. What matters is getting a return on your investment.

You control how much you spend, when and where your ads appear, who sees them and when you turn your ads off. Non-performing ads can be switched off at any time.

In this section I will outline the best way to use Facebook ads in order to get them working for your business. The basic structure for Facebook ads is as follows:

- Advertisers set goals. Facebook wants you to be very clear about what you want to achieve from your ad (see section 5.3).
- Advertisers identify audiences. You tell Facebook to whom you want your ad to be shown (see section 5.2).
- Advertisers create ads using a combination of media (images, videos) and text (see section 5.4.4).
- Facebook shows your ad to the advertiser's audience.
- Advertisers review ad performance and make informed decisions about future ads.

5.1 FACEBOOK AD MANAGER OVERVIEW

The Facebook Ads Manager can be found by selecting the drop-down menu at the top right hand corner of your profile. If you're a new advertiser this section will appear once you complete account set up. Select the option 'create ads' or 'manage ads'. (Fig. 5.1) By selecting 'manage ads' you will see an overview of all Facebook ad tools. (Fig. 5.2)

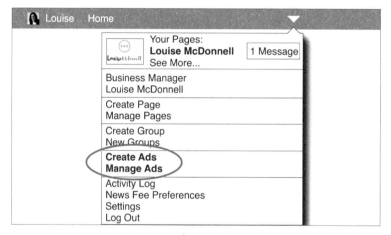

Fig. 5.1

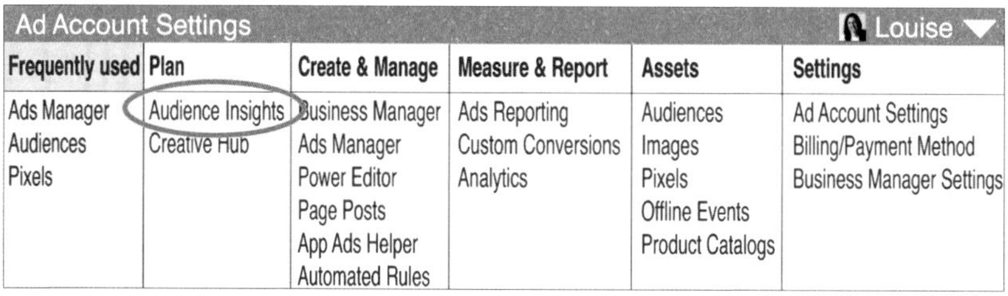

Fig. 5.2

Audience Insights

This is where you find detailed information about your audience, including:

- Demographics
- Relationship status
- Education level
- Job title
- Other pages that are likely to be relevant to your audience based on Facebook page likes
- Location
- Audience behaviour on Facebook
- Devices used.

Use this information to learn about the profile of *your* Facebook fans. When you can identify the profile of person who is most likely to like your page you can use this to create 'saved audiences' in Facebook ads.

Business Manager

You will find this tool useful if you're managing multiple pages or accounts and need to manage who has administrative access.

Ads Manager

This tool is most widely used by businesses that are starting to use Facebook ads. It enables you to set up, makes changes to and monitor the results of your ad campaigns.

Power Editor

This is a Google Chrome plugin generally used by larger Facebook ad users. It has more advanced features although recent changes have brought these tools closer in terms of functionality.

Pages Posts

This tool give you an overview of the scheduled, published and ad posts all in the one place. You can quickly switch between pages of which you are an administrator.

App Ads Helper

A tool to help you troubleshoot and fix any problems with your app ads.

Ads Reporting

Enables you to create and export reports from the Ads Manager.

Custom Conversions

This will track action on your website such as sales, enquires and page views without using the Facebook pixel.

Audiences

Where you can create and edit customer, lookalike and saved audiences.

Images

Where all the images previously used for your ads are stored. You can also upload new images.

Pixels

Where you can create a pixel for your account, set up conversion tracking and view results.

Offline Events

Use this tool to track when transactions occur in your physical store and other offline channels (for example, orders made over the phone) after people see or engage with your Facebook ad.

Product Catalogue

Enables you to upload a catalogue file of products you want to advertise.

Ad Accounts Settings

Where you can manage your account information, add and remove account advertisers, manage account notifications or deactivate your ad account.

Billing and Payment Methods

View your billing summary, manage your payment methods, set your account spending limit, view and print Facebook bills.

Business Manager Settings

Manage settings for the business manager in this section.

5.2 CREATING AUDIENCES FOR ADS

Facebook offers you the opportunity to create different audiences for your ads. The audience is who you want Facebook to show your ads to. You can select a different audience for every ad. Once you have designed your ad with good images or video and a compelling description, you can create different campaigns by selecting different audiences for your ad.

There is no limit on the number of audiences you can create. Once you have created an audience it is saved under your ad account and you can access it every time you are setting up a new ad regardless of whether you set up the ad on your phone or computer. My advice is to consider carefully how you name each of the audiences that you create. You will need to distinguish between multiple audiences in the future so don't be afraid to use long descriptive names.

There are three different types of audiences on Facebook: custom audiences, lookalike audiences and saved audiences.

Selecting the right audience can have a major influence on how well your ad performs. Consider how warm or cold the audience is (see section 2.4). Warm audiences know your brand (company) and are more likely to take the desired action from your ad (that is, like your page, complete a signup form, attend your event, download your app, purchase from your store, etc.).

Ultimately, you will never know how receptive or warm your audience is to your ad until you test it. Create different audiences, start using them for your ads and see what results you achieve. For example, if you create a campaign to grow page likes, you can use the ad creative (image and text) but show it to two different audiences, a custom audience, based on people who have visited your website, and a lookalike audience of people who have similar profiles to your existing page likes. Within 24 to 48 hours you will be able to see which audience is more receptive to your ad. If one ad is costing 50 cents per like and the other 10 cents, it's obvious which ad you need to switch off.

5.2.1 CUSTOM AUDIENCES

Reach people who have a relationship with your business, whether they are existing customers or people who have interacted with your business on Facebook or other platforms. These audiences are generally 'warm' to your brand. They already know you and are therefore more likely to do business with you than someone who is 'cold' to your brand.

You can associate a life time value (LTV) to your existing customers based on how valuable they are to your organiation. Customers with a high LTV may be expensive to acquire, but could lead to greater value over time.

There are a number of different ways to create custom audiences.

Customer Database

You can upload a customer database of email addresses or mobile numbers. Facebook will match your list with Facebook users to create a custom audience. How 'warm' this audience is depends on the quality of your database. If your list is made up of people who have purchased from you within the last twelve months, this is a 'warm' audience. Existing customers are about seven times more likely to do business with you in the future. If it's an older audience it may still be good but maybe not as warm. If your list is made up of people who entered a competition at a consumer show, it's probably cold so don't expect the same results.

Website Traffic

You can create audiences of people who have visited your website. To create these audiences you will need to place the Facebook pixel (see section 5.6), which is javascript code, on every page of your website. This code enables you to create the following audiences:

- People who have visited any page of your website. The code tracks people for up to 180 days. You can create different audiences based on when people visited your website. You can select between one and 180 days and create as many audiences as you want.

- People who visited specific pages on your website. So if someone visits a particular product or service page, you can create a product- or service-specific audience. If you have an ecommerce store you can create audiences based on people who have visited your shop pages.

- People who visited specific pages but not others. For example, this enables you to target people who visited product or services pages but not an enquiry or contact us page. For businesses with ecommerce stores it enables you to target people who visited shop pages but did not visit checkout pages.

- People who haven't visited for some time. This is a great way to get your brand in front of people who have visited your website in the past (within 180 days) but haven't been for a certain amount of time, for example, a month.

- You can also create audiences using a combination of conditions, for example, people who haven't visited specific pages in a certain number of days. Or people who have visited some pages but not others in a certain number of days.

- There are so many different applications to consider. If you have run a Google Adwords campaign in the last two weeks, you can re-market on Facebook to people who clicked through from your Google ad to your website. Or if you published a post on your Facebook page that linked to your website you can re-market to those people.

Create a Custom Audience from Your App

If you have developed an app for your business you can create a custom audience based on people who have used the app. You can create audiences based on actions taken, actions not taken, or a combination of actions.

Engagement on Facebook

You can also create an audience on Facebook based on people who have engaged with content on your Facebook page.

- If you have uploaded any native videos on Facebook (see section 4.4) you can create an audience of people who have viewed varying lengths of the video.

  ◇ You can select all viewers. On Facebook a view is three seconds or more.

  ◇ The second option is to select people who have viewed at least 10 seconds of your video. Facebook reports that people who watch 10 seconds of a video have a significant impact on ad recall, brand awareness and purchase intent.

  ◇ You can also create audiences based on the number of people who have watched 25 per cent, 50 per cent, 75 per cent or 95 per cent of the video. Obviously, the more of the video the audience has watched the 'warmer' they will be.

- If you have run any 'lead ads' (see section 5.3.2) you can create an audience of people who have opened any of your lead ads. There are a number of options to select from including:
  ◇ People who opened a lead ads form
  ◇ People who opened but did not submit the lead ad form
  ◇ People who opened the lead ad form and completed it.
- Create audiences based on people who have opened or clicked on any of the links in a 'canvas ad' (see section 5.4.3).
- Build audiences based on people who have visited or engaged with your Facebook page within the past year. Select from people who have:
  ◇ Visited your page
  ◇ Engaged with any post or ad
  ◇ Clicked on any call to action
  ◇ Sent a message to your page
  ◇ Saved your page or any post.

5.2.2 LOOKALIKE AUDIENCES

A lookalike audience is one that looks similar to your existing customers. It can be created using any of the custom audiences, or based on the existing fan base of your Facebook page.

A lookalike audience includes people who have the same demographics as the custom audience or Facebook fans, but who have not connected with your brand or your page.

Lookalike audiences are likely to be interested in your offerings but as yet they have not connected with you and are probably still 'cold' to your brand.

To create a lookalike audience:

1. Select the source of your custom audience (choose a customer audience, a conversion tracking pixel or a Facebook page).

2. Choose which location you wish to target.

3. Select the audience size. You will have the option of selecting between 1 and 10 per cent of the population in the countries selected, with the first being those who most closely match your source audience.

5.2.3 SAVED AUDIENCE

Saved audiences are created using demographic profiling such age, gender, relationship status and interests. It is advisable to use the information from customer personas to create saved audiences (see section 2.2).

To create a saved audience, use the following steps:

1. Give your audience a name.

2. Then select the location where the audience you propose to target is based. You can enter one or more countries, states/regions, cities, postal codes, addresses. You can also select locations that you want to exclude.

3. Select the age range for your audience.

4. You can select to target men, women or both genders.

5. In the 'detailed targeting' dialogue box you can narrow down your audience by including or excluding people based on their interests and behaviours. Simply start typing in this box and match with the options that Facebook offers. Try inserting job title, relationship status, pastime, etc.

5.3 CAMPAIGNS TO MEET DIFFERENT BUSINESS GOALS

The are three different campaign categories: awareness, consideration and conversion.

5.3.1 AWARENESS

Awareness campaigns all have the objective of increasing brand awareness with an audience. Types of ads include:

Reach

This objective lets you maximise the number of people who see your ads from your selected target audience. You can control frequency, limiting how many times people see your ads in a specific timeframe.

Brand Awareness Ads

By evaluating how much time people spend looking at different ads, Facebook can tell which people are more likely to watch and recall your ad, and optimise the campaign accordingly. It is PPM (pay per 1,000 impressions) rather than PPC (pay per click). The ads don't look any different – the difference is how Facebook optimises the campaigns (PPM).

5.3.2 CONSIDERATION ADS

Once you have created brand awareness with an audience you can begin to put specific propositions in front of them.

Traffic

This type of ad links to a page on a website external to Facebook. It can be your own website, blog, event page or any other webpage. It is used to raise awareness about a product or service, to promote blogs or articles or to raise attendance at events. Traffic ads are optimised in the newsfeed for link clicks. This means Facebook will get these ads in front of people from your target audience who are likely to click on the link.

Engagement Ads

There are three different ads to choose from in this objective:

1. Post Engagement. These are also called 'boost post' ads. Facebook will get this ad in front of people from your target audience who are likely to interact with the post by reacting (liking), commenting, sharing or clicking it.

2. Page Likes. The objective of these ads is to grow page likes. When someone likes your page you have a better chance of reaching them organically (when you update your page). You can also target them with boost posts (people who like your page). It's useful for remarketing to people who are interested in your brand. Potential customers need to hear about you between 9 and 17 times before they convert. Having an active page with high numbers of page likes also says something about your brand.

3. Event Responses. If you have created a Facebook event (see section 1.12) use this ad to encourage people to attend.

App Installs

Choose this ad to send people to the store where they can download or purchase your app.

Video Views

Choose this ad to get your video ad in front of people from your selected target audience who are most likely to watch it.

Lead Generation

Lead ads are designed for mobile phones. They make it easy for people to opt in from their phones and should be used for newsletter sign ups, offers, events, etc. When someone clicks on your lead ad, a form opens with the person's contact information automatically populated, based on the information they share with Facebook, like their name and email address. Filling in the form is as fast as two taps: one click on the ad to open the form and another to submit the auto-filled form. It's also possible to feed the information collected directly into your customer relationship management (CRM) system.

5.3.3 CONVERSION ADS

Conversion ads use the Facebook pixel code to trace the performance of sales ads. As noted earlier, the Facebook pixel is a piece of JavaScript code for your website that enables you to measure, optimise and build audiences for your ad campaigns. Using the Facebook pixel, you can leverage the actions people take on your website across devices to inform future campaigns.

Conversions

Get people to take valuable actions on your website or app, such as watching a demo or purchasing a product. The Facebook pixel measures and optimises ads for conversions. This means that Facebook will show your conversion ad to people who are most likely to convert. Use warm audiences for conversion ads as they are most likely to convert.

Product Catalogue Sales

To run product catalogue ads you must first set up a product catalogue in the catalogue manager. You can create a catalogue by uploading a product file or linking to your website. Facebook currently supports the following file types: CSV, TSV, RSS XML, or ATOM XML. This enables you to automatically create ads for products in your catalogue. The ads are targeted at people who have already shown an interest in your products.

Store Visits

This is used to promote multiple store locations to people nearby. To use this objective you must first set up your business locations in business manager.

5.4 HOW CAMPAIGNS ARE STRUCTURED

Facebook ads have a three layer structure. Each campaign must have one objective. Campaigns can have one or more ad sets as well as one or more ads. (Fig. 5.3)

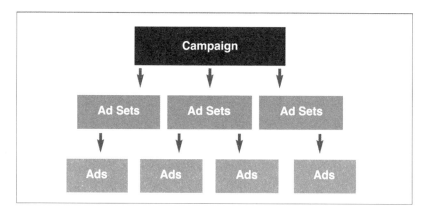

Fig. 5.3

5.4.1 CAMPAIGNS

Facebook will automatically give your campaign a name relating to the objective selected. When creating a campaign you can edit the name Facebook has created to one that will mean something to you in a few months' time. If all your campaigns have generic names it makes it harder to compare them in the future.

5.4.2 AD SETS

The ad set contains details of the audience you are targeting (see section 5.3), placements, budget and the schedule of when the ads are running.

Audience

The 'audience' is the people you want Facebook to display your ads to. You can select from custom, lookalike and saved audiences (see section 5.2).

Placement

In the 'placements' section you can select which devices you wish your ads to be shown on. Choose between mobile or desktop on Facebook, Instagram or Audience Networks. There are also advanced options to select between Android and iOS.

If you are running video ads you have the option of showing them between suggested videos in the video player.

Platforms

Facebook ads can also run on Instagram as well as on third party networks. It is possible to select which platforms you wish to have your ads running in this section. (Fig. 5.4)

Budget and Schedule

Select from a daily or a lifetime budget. If you want to schedule your ads to run at certain times of the day, then you must select lifetime budget.

You can create multiple ad sets for each campaign using a variable of the elements in the ads set. This is a useful way of testing different audiences, platforms, devices, etc. within the same campaign. Remember to give each ad set a name that you can easily distinguish between.

5.4.3 Ads

Create your ad visuals by selecting media (images or video), text and links. Each campaign can have multiple ads so you can test between different visuals and text to see what appeals most to your target audience.

Placements
Show your ads to the right people in the right places.

○ **Automatic Placements (Recommended)**
Your ads will automatically be shown to your audience in the places they're likely to perform best. Learn more.

◉ **Edit placements**
Removing placements may reduce the number of people you reach and may make it less likely that you'll meet your goals. Learn more.

Device Types	Mobile Only ▼
Platforms	
	ADVANCED OPTIONS
Specific Mobile Devices & Operating Systems	All Mobile Devices ▼

Fig. 5.4

Media

The campaign objective dictates the media formats available to you for creating your ad. Choose between:

- **Carousel**: Choose this option to create an ad with two or more scrollable images or video. The recommended size for Carousel images is 1080 × 1080 pixels with little or no overlaid text.

- **Single image ads**. You can have six ads using different images. For single image ads the recommended image specification is 1200 x 628 pixels.

- **Single video ads**. The recommended format for video ads is MOV or .MP4 files that have a resolution of at least 720p. The maximum size is 2.3 GB max with a wide screen aspect (16:9). The maximum time for video ads on Facebook is 60 minutes and for Instagram is 60 seconds.

- **Slideshow**: Upload up to 10 images to create a looped video ad. It is recommended that images are widescreen ratio (16:9). This is an easy way of creating a video effect using images.

- **Collection**: This format combines a video, slideshow or image with product images taken from a product catalogue or mobile.
- **Canvas**: A combination of video, image carousels, text and buttons that displays in full screen on mobile devices.

The images you use can have a big impact on the success of your ad. Spend time selecting your images and use tools like Canva to resize images to the recommended size as outlined by Facebook. Image sizes on Facebook are constantly changing so check the recommended image spec before you spend time resizing images. When you are setting up your ad, the recommended specs are displayed predominantly on the screen.

Here are some tips for selecting what images to use:

1. Use images with little or no text. In the past ad images with over 20 per cent text were automatically disapproved by Facebook. In 2016 Facebook relaxed this rule but you should still use as little text as possible. Ads containing images with little or no text tend to be more successful.

2. Use images with one focal point or subject that draws the viewers' attention immediately. Remember, people are scrolling quickly through their news feeds so you need to 'stop them as they scroll'. For example, a hotel might want to use a stunning image showing the hotel in the distance, but when it appears as part of a Facebook ad it will just be a dot on the screen making the image ineffective.

3. Where possible, integrate your company logo, font and brand colours. Make it easy for potential customers to identify your company and its products in a crowded marketplace. Colour has a major impact on brand identification so find out the HEX or RGB references for your brand and use them consistently on all visuals. Your graphic designer should be able to assist in providing these references. If

not, you can use free tools like ColorPic by Iconico.com or ColorZilla for Google Chrome to identify brand colours.

4. Use people. Images with people who look like your target audience can be effective. If you are targeting retired people, consider using an image with an older person. Likewise, if you are selling children's products, using a child's image makes sense.

5. Use high quality images. Blurry, dark images will go unnoticed in the news feed and may have a negative impact on your brand. Stock images can work well as they are high quality images and include any subject, location, emotion or colour. If you are selling products, your supplier will have high quality stock images available for instant use. If you are employing a photographer to capture images consider all the different sizes you will require for your website, email marketing, social media, etc. Remember to integrate your logo on photo shoots as well.

6. Think outside the box. Images that are different capture attention. Remember your goal is to get your ad to stand out and to appeal to your target audience. Unusual images can achieve this.

7. Test. The only way to know what will appeal to your target audience is to test. Try different images using the same ad headline and description to see which one performs the best.

Ad Text

It's important when creating your ad to choose your headline and ad description well.

*   What will appeal to your target audience?
*   How can you capture their attention?
*   What will resonate with your audience?

- Remember to sell benefits not just features.
- What's the most important aspect of the ad that will be useful to your ideal customer?
- What problems are you solving? What needs are you fulfilling?
- Can you add credibility by including examples of awards, accolades or social proof?
- Use local town names if relevant.
- Use month references too if relevant.
- Can you incentivise the reader to act sooner than later by offering an early bird offer or limited availability?
- It's always advisable to include a 'call to action' – what you want the reader to do next (call, email, shop, etc.).

Creating text for your ad is not easy. It's not something you'll do well if you're under pressure for time. What can you say that's going to appeal to your customer? Remember: *it's not about what you want to say, it's about what matters to them.*

5.5 HOW TO CREATE FACEBOOK ADS

In this section we will look at how to:

1. Boost an ad from the news feed
2. How to create an ad using Facebook Ads Manager.

5.5.1 CREATING A POST ENGAGEMENT (BOOST POST) FROM THE NEWS FEED

The simplest way to create a Facebook ad is to run a boosted post from your page's news feed. Simply select the 'boost post' button which is found underneath your post.

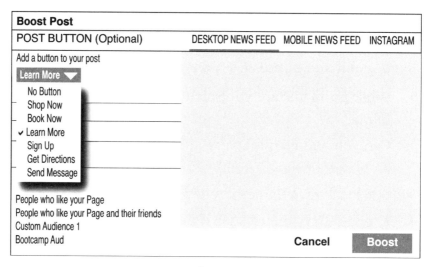

Fig. 5.5

As you can see from the image above, you can add a 'call to action' to your ad by selecting the 'post button'. Choose from:

- Shop now
- Book now
- Learn more
- Sign up
- Get directions
- Send message.

Including a 'call to action' on your ad makes it obvious to the reader what you want them to do next.

Then you select the audience you wish to target. When you boost a post from your page the three audience options available to you are:

- People who like your page
- People who like your page and their friends
- People you choose through targeting.

People Who Like Your Page

The people who like your page are already 'warm' to your brand. At some point you impressed them enough that they liked your page. They are likely to have seen your posts in their news feed. They are a warmer prospect than someone who has never heard of your business or seen your page. Use this option when you publish a post and want to guarantee that your existing fans see it.

People Who Like Your Page and Their Friends

Friends of people who like your page are likely to have the same demographics and general interests as your page fans. People are also more likely to deal with businesses that their friends use.

People You Choose through Targeting

You can select an audience that you have created and saved in the past (see section 5.2) or you can create a new audience. You can create an audience based on gender, age, location and interest. There are more options available when you create audiences using the Facebook Ads Manager or Power Editor. Using these tools you can make your audiences more specific by excluding some locations and interests. They also offer the ability to target people by language and using advanced combinations of people who are connected to your page, app or event.

5.5.2 CREATING AN AD USING ADS MANAGER

You will find the Ads Manager by selecting 'create ads' or 'manage ads' from the dropdown menu at the top right of your Facebook account. Upon selecting 'create ad' you will see the campaign overview page. (Fig. 5.6)

Select the campaign objective that will help you achieve your overall goal. There are ten objectives displayed, with an additional three objectives under the engagement option.

Once you have selected a marketing objective (choose from the 10 shown), Facebook will give you the option to name your campaign. Using detailed campaign names will enable you to easily identify one campaign from another in the future. Consider including the month or the year in the campaign name. If you have more than one Facebook page, include the name of the page the campaign is for.

What's your marketing objective?		
Awareness	**Consideration**	**Conversion**
Brand awareness	Traffic	Conversions
Reach	Engagement	Product catalog sales
	App installs	Store visits
	Video views	
	Lead generation	

Fig. 5.6

In the example below, I have selected to create a campaign to grow my page likes, so I selected 'page likes'. (Fig. 5.7)

Fig. 5.7

In the above example, the default campaign name is 'engagement'. Change this campaign name to something more specific like 'page likes campaign February 2018'. Once I select 'continue' I am brought to the 'ad set' page. In this section I select the page I wish to promote (this will only apply if there is more than one page), the audience I want Facebook to target, where I want my ads to be placed, how much I wish to spend and my ad schedule. (Fig. 5.8)

Fig. 5.8

Any of my custom or lookalike audiences will appear if I start typing the audience name in the 'custom audience' dialogue box.

To select a 'saved audience' simply select the 'use a saved audience' drop down menu and your saved audiences will appear. (Fig. 5.9)

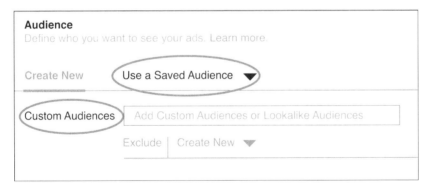

Fig. 5.9

In this example I have selected a custom audience using the Facebook pixel to create an audience based on people who have visited my website in the last 180 days. I know this is a warm audience that is more likely to 'like my page'. (Fig. 5.10)

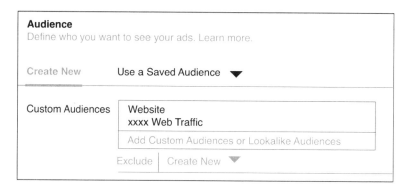

Fig. 5.10

Under 'placements' you can select 'automatic placements' where Facebook will show your ads on the platforms that they believe are most likely to get the best results. Or you can select 'edit placements' and select from Facebook, Instagram, Audience Networks and mobile/desktop devices.

If your audience are Instagram users then running ads on Instagram is likely to be good for your brand. The best way to find out is to run some ads and test the results.

In this example, as the campaign objective selected is to grow page likes, it's not possible to show the ads on Instagram or third party networks. (Fig. 5.11)

In the 'budget & schedule' section you can define how much you wish to spend and when you would like your ads to appear.

Under budget you have the option to choose between daily and lifetime budget. If you want to create a schedule for your ads (for example, between 8.00 am and 10.00 am every day) then you have to select lifetime budget. In this example I'm choosing 'daily budget'. I'm going to spend €10 a day for five days growing my page likes. That's a total cost of €50 plus vat.

Under 'schedule' if you don't select an end date for the campaign it will automatically set your campaign up to run for one month. (Fig. 5.12)

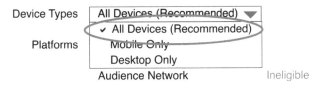

Placements
Show your ads to the right people in the right places.

○ **Automatic Placements (Recommended)**

⊙ **Edit placements**

Device Types | All Devices (Recommended) ▼

               ✓ All Devices (Recommended)

Platforms   Mobile Only

               Desktop Only

        Audience Network   Ineligible

Fig. 5.11

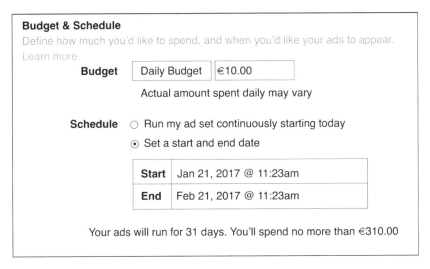

Budget & Schedule
Define how much you'd like to spend, and when you'd like your ads to appear.
Learn more.

Budget   Daily Budget   €10.00

              Actual amount spent daily may vary

Schedule   ○ Run my ad set continuously starting today

            ⊙ Set a start and end date

Start	Jan 21, 2017 @ 11:23am
End	Feb 21, 2017 @ 11:23am

Your ads will run for 31 days. You'll spend no more than €310.00

Fig. 5.12

When selecting the end date, be careful that the date hasn't already jumped on one month. Remember to go back a month to the start date and count the number days you wish to run the campaign from there. Many businesses have run campaigns for one month and five days rather than five days as they didn't notice that the end date had already jumped on one month.

Under advanced options you have the option to manually set what you are willing to bid for each ad result. In this example the ad result is a 'page like'.

All ads on Facebook compete for ad space. The higher your bid the more likely your ad will be shown. However there are other factors which influence this like ad quality and relevance to the target audience.

When creating your Facebook ad, you can set your bid automatically or manually.

Automatic Bid

By selecting this option, Facebook decides the bid amount for you. In this case, Facebook spends your ad budget with the goal of maximising the campaign object (a page like). If you are unsure how much to bid, Facebook recommends choosing this option.

Manual Bid

This option enables you to tell Facebook the maximum amount you are willing to spend to achieve the result you want. Facebook suggests a bid which will change depending on the audiences you have selected. (Fig. 5.13)

Optimisation for Ad Delivery	**Page Likes** – We'll deliver your ads to the right people to help you get more Page likes at the lowest cost.
Bid Amount	○ **Automatic** – Let us set the bid that helps you get the most Page likes at the best price. ⊙ **Manual** – Enter a bid based on what Page likes are worth to you. ☐ per Page like Suggested bid: €0.42 EUR (€0.35-€0.53)
When You Get Charged	Impression More Options
Ad Scheduling	Run ads all the time More Options

Fig. 5.13

Under the option 'when you get charged', you can select how you get charged. In this example the two options are by 'impression' and by 'page like'. If you're new to Facebook ads stick with the default setting. The more advertising you do the more in tune you will become to bid amounts and cost per impression/page like.

Under 'ad scheduling' you can choose from running your ads all the time or running them on a schedule. Remember that ad scheduling will only work if you have selected a lifetime budget. It's worth noting that the ads are served in your audience's time zone. (Fig. 5.14)

Fig. 5.14

Under delivery type you can choose from 'standard' delivery, which will show your ads throughout the day, or 'accelerated' delivery, which will show your ads as quickly as possible.

Next, you need to give your 'ad set' a name before you can continue. Because campaigns can be made up of more than one ad set (audience, placement, budget & schedule) it's important to name your ad set carefully to facilitate how you interpret ad performance.

Once the ad set is set up the next stage of your campaign is to create the ad itself. As I have selected the campaign objective to grow page likes the format options that are presented to me are:

- Single image ad
- Single video
- Slideshow (a video ad using up to 10 images).

I have decided to select a single image ad. I can choose up to six different images that will create six different ads. It's important to choose images that are eye-catching and the right size (see section 5.4.3).

Facebook automatically pulls in your page cover image but you don't have to use it. You can upload new images or browse images that you have used before that are in your image library. Facebook also gives you the option to use free stock images. Remember that the quality of your images has a big impact on the success of your ad, including the cost and campaign outcome.

For my campaign I have selected six images using a combination I have created using Canva and stock images.

Write your ad text with your target audience in mind. In this example I am targeting small businesses in a 50 kilometre radius so I give my ad local context. It's more likely to pop out at them. I also focus on what I can do for them as this approach usually provides a better outcome for ads like this.

Facebook gives you a preview of your ad using all the selected images (one ad per image). It also gives you a preview of how the ads will look on desktop and mobile news feed, feature phone and desktop right column. (Fig. 5.15)

It's possible to click into any of the sections on the left hand side (campaign, ad set and ad) to edit any element of the campaign before placing your order. To complete the process select the 'place order' button at the bottom right hand side of the screen. (Fig. 5.16)

Fig. 5.15

Fig. 5.16

5.6 THE FACEBOOK PIXEL

According to Facebook:

> *The Facebook pixel is a piece of JavaScript code for your website that enables you to measure, optimise and build audiences for your ad campaigns.*

The Facebook pixel enables you to:

• Create customer and lookalike audiences for your Face-book ads based on people who have visited your website, added products to a shopping cart or purchased a product.

- Measure cross-device conversions. See how your customers are moving between devices (for example, smart phones, tablets, desktops) before they convert.

- Get your ads in front of people who are most likely to take action such as to purchase or fill out a form.

- Run dynamic product ads. This enables you to remarket to people who have visited product pages on your website.

- Access Audience Insights. Get rich insights about the people who visit your website.

5.6.1 How to Set up the Facebook Pixel

You can only set up one pixel per ad account. If you have multiple websites and wish to create different audiences for each, you will need to set up a different pixel for each one. Similarly, if you are managing Facebook ads for another business or organisation, it's best if they set up an ad account and then make you an administrator of it. You can add administrators under 'ad account settings'.

1. Go to your Facebook pixel tab in Ads Manager.

2. Click 'create a pixel'. (Fig. 5.17)

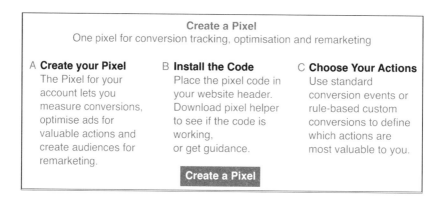

Fig. 5.17

3. Enter a name for your pixel. You can have only one pixel per ad account, so choose a name that represents your business. (Fig. 5.18)

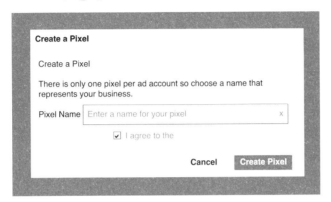

Fig. 5.18

4. Note: You can change the name of the pixel later from the Facebook pixel tab.

5. Check the box to accept the terms.

6. Click create pixel.

The pixel is shown below. (Fig. 5.19)

```
<!-- Pixel Code -->
<script>
!function(f,b,e,v,n,t,s){if(f.fbq)return;n=f.fbq=function(){n.callMethod?
n.callMethod.apply(n,arguments):n.queue.push(arguements)};if(!f._fbq)f._fbq=n;
n.push=n;n.loaded=!0;n.version='2.0';nqueue=[];t=b.createElement(e);t.async=!0:
t.src=v;s=b.getElementsByTagName(e)[0];s.parentNode.insertBefore(t,s)}(window,
document,'script','https://connect.net/en_US/fbevents.js'):
fbq)'init','100xxxxxxxxxx '); // Insert your pixel ID here.
fbq('track','PageView');
</script>
(noscript><img height="1"width="1"style="display:none"
src= "https://www.xxxxxxxx.com/tr?id=100xxxxxxxxxx &ev=PageView&noscript=1"
/></noscript>
<!--DO NOT MODIFY-->
<!--End Pixel Code-->
```

Fig. 5.19

The Facebook pixel has three main functions:

1. It enables you to build custom audiences based on people who have visited your website.
2. It optimises ads for conversions.
3. It tracks ecommerce conversions and lets you know which ads are working.

The base code must be installed within the code on every page of your website.

5.6.2 USING THE FACEBOOK PIXEL BASE CODE

If you install the base code only you can use it to create custom audiences and track custom conversions.

Using the Pixel to Create Custom Audiences

A custom audience can be created from people who have visited all or certain pages of your website. It tracks visitors to your website for up to 180 days.

To create a custom audience using the standard pixel code, go to the audience section of Facebook ads.

Select 'create audiences' and then select 'custom audiences'. Then select the option website traffic. You must have the pixel installed on your website before you can do this. The pixel will only track visitors once installed. So if you installed the pixel seven days ago, you can only create an audience based on the traffic that has been monitored since then.

You can create multiple audiences based on when people have visited your website. If you have been running a specific campaign (email, radio, affiliate, etc.) driving traffic to your website over the last week, you can create an audience to remarket to the people who visited your website as a result of that campaign. The maximum number of days you can track people to your website is 180 days.

You can create audiences based on people who have visited specific pages on your website. If you have an ecommerce store you can track people who browsed your store. Or if you're running an event, you can track people who visited the event page. Perhaps you've written a blog about a particular subject. If so, you can track people who visited that blog page.

There is also the opportunity to create audiences based on people who have visited specific pages but not others. For ecommerce stores you can create audiences based on people who have visited your store pages, but did not visit a checkout page. So you know they were interested enough to browse your store, but did not purchase. Similarly, you could create an audience of people who visited an event page but did not visit the event registration page. You know they were interested enough in the event to visit the page, but didn't register at the time.

It is also possible to create an audience based on people who haven't visited in a certain amount of time. This is based on people who have visited your site within the last 180 days but haven't returned for specific amount of time, which you can set.

It's also possible to refine your audiences using combination of any of the conditions above.

Using the Pixel Code to Track Custom Conversions

You can track custom conversions on your website without adding any additional code to the base pixel code on your website. (In section 5.6.3 we will look at the event code where you can modify the base code on certain pages to track specific actions.)

This option is generally used by people who can't add a standard event (see section 5.6.3) to their websites. Custom conversions enable you to track conversations on your website using URL rules.

The URL is the specific address for an individual page on your website. So the URL for my home page is www.louisemcdonnell. com and the URL for my courses page is www.louisemcdonnell.

com/courses. When people make purchases from a website the URL generally says something like www.yourwebsite.com/ thankyou. Facebook enables you to track conversions on your website by counting the number of times people visit these 'thank you' pages. In order to use this you will need to check how your website is set up and to identify the specific URLs of the pages you want to track.

It's also possible to add a conversion value when you're setting up customer conversions on your website. This is only effective if all products and services being sold on your website have the same value.

In the example below I have created a custom conversion to track sales of one of the courses on my website. (Fig. 5.20)

URL Option	How you'd set your rule	Equivalent Standard Event
URL Equals	www.mywebsiteurl.com/thankyou.php	Purchase
URL Contain	/thankyou.php	Purchase

Fig. 5.20

As you can see I have copied and pasted the URL that people arrive at once they have paid for one of my courses. I have selected the category 'purchase'. (Fig. 5.21)

Other categories available are:

• View content

• Search

• Add to cart

• Add to wishlist

• Initiate checkout

• Add payment info

• Purchase

- Lead
- Complete registration
- Other.

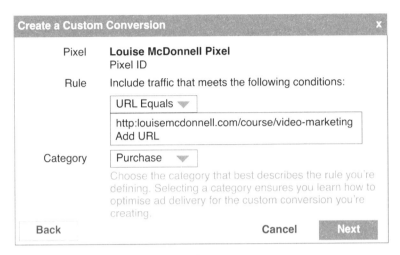

Fig. 5.21

On the next page give your custom conversion a name and a value if you wish. It's important that you choose a name that you will recognise later, especially if you are setting up many different custom conversions. (Fig. 5.22)

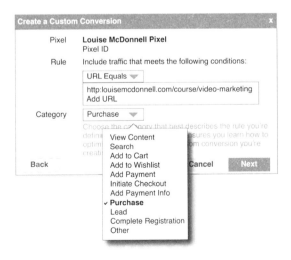

Fig. 5.22

This custom conversion is then available to use the next time you are setting up conversion ads.

Using Custom Conversions to Split Standard Events

If you are using standard events but would like more detailed information, custom conversions can help, for example, if you are using a standard event to track 'view content' actions across the website. Custom conversions can be set up to give you a better breakdown of what product categories are being viewed.

In the example below, this custom conversion will allow the advertiser to track views of a video course on its website. (Fig. 5.23)

Fig. 5.23

Using Custom Conversion Events

If you're already using standard events (see section 5.6.3) but find that you need more customisation, custom conversions can help. For example, if you're a clothing business and you've been using the view content standard event for all your products, but want to optimise for separate categories, you can split these out into custom conversions.

When creating your custom conversion, use the URL rules to create conversions for your different categories. In the example below, the URL rule allows for your ad to optimise only for people who view men's clothing.

5.6.3 USING THE PIXEL CODE TO TRACK STANDARD EVENTS

When you create a Facebook pixel for your ad account it looks as shown in Fig. 5.19. Facebook give you the option of adding an additional piece of code to this pixel to track nine standard events on your website. (Fig. 5.24)

Website action	Standard event code
View content	fbq("track", "ViewContent");
Search	fbq("track", "Search");
Add to cart	fbq("track", "AddToCart");
Add to wishlist	fbq("track", "AddToWishlist");
Initiate checkout	fbq("track", "InitiateCheckout");
Add payment info	fbq("track", "AddPaymentInfo");
Make purchase	fbq("track", "Purchase", {value: '0.00', currency: EURO);
Lead	fbq("track", "Lead");
Complete registration	fbq("track", "CompleteRegistration");

Fig. 5.24

If you want to track when registrations are made on your website you add 'fbq ('track', 'CompleteRegistration');' to the pixel code, but only on the relevant page on your website. In this example it would be the page that visitors to your website arrive at once they have completed registration.

As shown on the following page, the code is added after fbq('track', 'PageView') and before </script>. (Fig. 5.25)

You can also send these instructions to your web developer and they will do this for you.

Once any standard events have been saved on your website you will be able to use these to track conversions on ads. This will track not only the number of conversions but also the value as the sale amount is taken from the website transaction.

```
<-- Pixel Code -->
<script>
!function(f,b,e,v,n,t,s){if(f.fbq)return;n=f.fbq=function(){n.callMethod?
n,callMethod.apply(n,arguments):n.queue.push(arguments)};if(!f._fbq)f._fbq=n;
n.push=n;n.loaded=!0;n.version='2.0';n.queue=[];t=b.createElement(e);t.async=!0;
t.src=v;s=b.getElementsByTagName(e)[0];s.parentNode.insertBefore(t,s)}(window,
document,'script','https://connect.net/en_US/fbevent.js');
fbq('init','100xxxxxxxxxx');//Insert your pixel ID here.
fbq('track','PageView');
        fbq('track','CompleteRegistration');
</script>
<noscript><img height="1" width="1" style="display:none"
src="https://tr?id=100xxxxxxxxxx &ev=PageView&noscript=1"
/></noscript>
<!--DO NOT MODIFY-->
<!-- End Pixel Code -->
```

Fig. 5.25

5.7 INTERPRETING RESULTS

Facebook provides comprehensive reporting so you can review how your ads have performed and make informed decisions about future ads.

The first question you should be asking yourself is whether your ad achieved its objective. If you boosted a post to grow awareness about a particular product or service, did more people (from your target audience) enquire about it? Did you track where the product enquiries/sales emanated from? How many can be attributed to Facebook? How many people engaged with the boosted post? How many comments, reactions and shares did it receive? Was there a link in the post and if so how many people clicked on it?

If you ran an ad campaign to grow page likes, how many likes did your campaign generate? How much did each new page like cost? Did one image outperform others? Did one ad description resonate more than others?

If you ran a campaign to send traffic to a page on your website (like an event page or a product or service page), how many people clicked through? And how many people converted?

If you ran a campaign to increase add installations or video views, how much did each view/installation cost? And what was it worth to your business?

While Facebook offers powerful reporting tools I recommend that businesses also tune into offline events. I have regularly seen campaigns generate sales which cannot be directly linked to a Facebook ad campaign. Product sales increase while the Facebook ads are running, but only a percentage of those sales can be linked to the ad through Facebook's reporting system. But after the ad stops showing, if product sales revert back to their normal levels we can assume that the ad has generated the additional sales. This often happens when people see an ad on Facebook using a mobile device and then use a different device (perhaps a laptop) at a later time to purchase the product. In this example, the individual is not logged on to Facebook on the device on which they made the purchase, therefore Facebook cannot track this event (sale) in their reports.

5.7.1 Campaign Performance

Facebook provides statistics on how campaigns perform using the same structure as ad setup. The first level of statistics are at campaign level. The default fields for reporting are:

- Results (see Fig. 5.26 – 1)
- Reach (see Fig. 5.26 – 2)
- Costs (see Fig. 5.26 – 3)
- Amount spent (see Fig. 5.26 – 4).

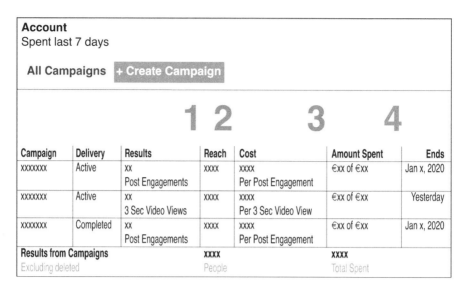

Account
Spent last 7 days

All Campaigns   + Create Campaign

1 2   3   4

Campaign	Delivery	Results	Reach	Cost	Amount Spent	Ends
xxxxxxx	Active	xx Post Engagements	xxxx	xxxx Per Post Engagement	€xx of €xx	Jan x, 2020
xxxxxxx	Active	xx 3 Sec Video Views	xxxx	xxxx Per 3 Sec Video View	€xx of €xx	Yesterday
xxxxxxx	Completed	xx Post Engagements	xxxx	xxxx Per Post Engagement	€xx of €xx	Jan x, 2020
Results from Campaigns Excluding deleted			xxxx People		xxxx Total Spent	

Fig. 5.26

Results

This is the number of actions as a result of your ad. The 'action' relates to the type of campaign objective you selected. So, for example, if you have run a campaign to grow page likes the action reported will relate to the number of new page likes. If you ran a conversion campaign to boost sales on your website, the action reported on will relate to conversions.

Reach

The reach is the number of people who saw your ad at least once. This is different to impressions which is the number of times your ad appeared in the news feed (one person could have seen your ad multiple times).

Cost

The cost is the average cost per result for your ad.

Amount Spent

This is the total amount spent to date on what was committed to the campaign.

Ends

This is the date on which your campaign will finish.

Additional reporting fields can be added by selecting from the 'performance' drop down menu above the table.

Performance at Ad Set Level

On clicking on a campaign link, you get a breakdown of how each ad set in your campaign has performed. If you have only used one ad set this is what you will see. Again, the standard performance reporting fields are results, reach, cost, budget and amount spent. (Fig. 5.27)

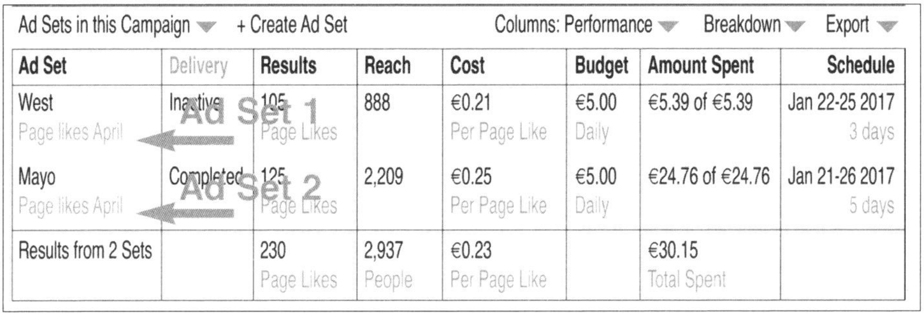

Ad Set	Delivery	Results	Reach	Cost	Budget	Amount Spent	Schedule
West Page likes April	Inactive	105 Page Likes	888	€0.21 Per Page Like	€5.00 Daily	€5.39 of €5.39	Jan 22-25 2017 3 days
Mayo Page likes April	Completed	125 Page Likes	2,209	€0.25 Per Page Like	€5.00 Daily	€24.76 of €24.76	Jan 21-26 2017 5 days
Results from 2 Sets		230 Page Likes	2,937 People	€0.23 Per Page Like		€30.15 Total Spent	

Fig. 5.27

At the top of the page there are three tabs: performance, demographics and placement. The performance tab gives a graphical representation of the standard reporting fields. A demographics tab gives a breakdown of the profile of people who have engaged with your ad. You can see a breakdown of gender, age and cost per result. (Fig. 5.28)

A placement tab gives a breakdown of what network the ads have been displayed on. It gives a breakdown between Facebook, Instagram and Audience Networks. There is also a breakdown of devices your ads have appeared on. By noting what platforms and devices your ads perform best on, you can make more informed decisions about future campaigns.

Fig. 5.28

Performance of Each Ad

Click on an ad set to see how each ad is performing. Again you will see a breakdown for each ad under three tabs – performance, demographics and placement. If you have used multiple ads (using different images, videos and description, it's possible to see what's working best with your target audience. (Fig. 5.29)

Ads in this Ad Set ▼	+ Create Ad Set			Columns: Performance ▼	Breakdown ▼	Export ▼
Ad Name	Delivery	**Results**	**Reach**	**Cost**	**Amount Spent**	**Relevance**
Image 2 Page likes April	Not Delivering Ad Set Competed	xxx Page Likes	xxx	xxx Per Page Like	xxx	9
Image 3 Page likes April	Not Delivering	**Multiple Ads**		xxx Per Page Like	xxx	10
Image 4 Page likes April	Not Delivering Ad Set Competed	xxx Page Likes	xxx	xxx Per Page Like	xxx	9
Results from 3 Ads		xxx Page Likes	xxx People	xxx Per Page Like	xxx Total Spent	

Fig. 5.29

Here is an explanation of the most commonly user terms:

• Reach: The number of people who saw your ad.

• Impressions: The number of times your ad was viewed.

- Cost: The average you paid for each action (the action related to the campaign objective. For example, if the objective is to grow page likes, the action is the number of new page likes).

- Budget: The amount you are willing to pay for each ad set.

- Clicks: Clicks on the ad.

- CTR: Click through rate (clicks/impresssions).

- CPC: Cost per click.

- Relevance: All ads with over 500 impressions are given a 'relevant score'. This metric is only available at ad level (not ad sets campaigns). It is a mark out of 10 based on how well your target audience is responding to your ad. It only appears after ads have received more than 500 impressions. An ad with a low relevant score will cost more to achieve its objective.

It's possible to turn off ads that are not performing and to allocate more of your budget to ads that are achieving better results.

5.8 ADVERTISING STRATEGY

If you are going to start investing in Facebook ads make sure it is part of a wider business strategy. Spending money on ads on an ad hoc basis may limit the success of campaigns and result in poor return on investment.

In general, in order for someone to do business with you they have to have the following:

- Requirement for your products/services. Someone may have a requirement for what you sell but might not be ready to purchase at that moment. Several factors may influence this like having the funds available to spend, having the time, personal issues, schedule, etc.

- Purchase intent – they need to be ready to purchase.

- Brand awareness – Does the prospect know you? If they've never heard of you or know anyone who has used you the likelihood of them doing business with you is low. However, if they are warm to your brand through personal recommendations or seeing high quality posts on your page or reading five star reviews there is more likelihood they will consider doing business with you.

- Repeat business – Satisfied customers are more likely to repeat their business with you. Customers that are blown away with you tend to refer friends and family to you.

5.8.1 IDENTIFY YOUR BUSINESS GOALS

If you are clear about what you want to achieve and by when, you can start making a plan incorporating your pages content, timing of posts and then link this with Facebook ads.

For example, a business may have product sales goals for specific target audiences. A hairdresser, let's call her Mary, has a good trade with customers in their thirties and forties and wishes to attract females in their twenties. Mary sets a goal that in a two month period she will receive 20 appointments from females in their twenties through her Facebook page.

5.8.2 CREATE POSTING AND AD STRATEGY

Once the business goal is set, then a strategy can be put in place for achieving it. Let's consider our example of Mary the Hairdresser. In order to achieve her goal, Mary needs to come up with content on her page that will appeal to her target audience.

- She may publish 'get the look' posts where she imitates hair styles of celebrities in their twenties. In her post, she shows the celebrity as well as a photo showing her work.

- She may post tips and advice that relate to new fads that people in their twenties are likely to be interested in.
- She may create a series of blog posts on her website with content that would appeal to the target audience.
- She may encourage some members of her staff in their twenties to create video tips. By doing this her target audience will identify with her and her staff.

She is introducing her business to an audience that is largely 'cold' to her brand. Mary will use the content on her page to 'warm' up this audience. The more times Mary can get good quality, relevant content in front of this audience the 'warmer' they will be to her brand.

5.8.3 WARM VS COLD AUDIENCE

In section 2.5 we looked at creating a sales funnel and moving customers along the loyalty ladder with the ultimate aim of making them customer advocates. To reach this new audience Mary can do a number of things:

- She can invite people she knows who are female and in their twenties to like her page.
- She can ask any of her staff who are administrators on her page to invite their friends (who are female and in their twenties) to like the page.
- She can ask all other staff members (not admins of the page) to share the page on their personal profiles.
- She can run Facebook ads using the following audiences
  - ◇ People who like her page (*warm audience)*
  - ◇ People who like her page and their friends (*warm audience)*
  - ◇ People who have watched videos on the page that were created to appeal to the target audience (*warm audience)*

◇ People who have visited the blog article pages of her website (using the Facebook pixel – see section 5.6) (*warm audience*)

◇ Saved target audiences living within a 30k radius aged between twenty and thirty who aren't connected to her page (*cold audience*).

• She could run the following campaigns using the audiences above:

◇ A campaign to grow page likes. Remember, someone needs to hear about you 9 to 17 times before they'll do business with you. So if Mary can attract them as a page like for her business she has the opportunity to reach them every time she publishes a post on her page. The higher the quality of the content and the more relevant it is to the target audience the more she will warm them up. (*Use this with cold audiences.*)

◇ Post engagement/boost posts. She can ensure that her target audience sees her content by boosting the post to reach them in their news feeds. (*Can be used with cold and warm audiences.*)

◇ Send people to a destination off Facebook. Mary can use Traffic Ads to drive traffic to the blog posts on her website. The blog articles with content of high relevance to her target audience will 'warm' them to her brand. If she has the Facebook pixel installed on her website she can then remarket to them by creating an audience of people who have visited that specific page on her website. (*Can be used with cold audiences to warm them up, and to further impress warm audiences.*)

◇ She could send people to a landing page on her website that is designed specifically to convert them. The landing page needs to clearly set out the benefits to the prospect, what the proposition is (what Mary is offering) and a clear call to action. (*In general, landing pages are more successful with warmer audiences but can work with cold audiences.*)

◇ Facebook offer: Create an offer that will appeal to her target audience. Limit its availability and the duration for better results. (*More likely to be used by warmer audiences.*)

◇ Increase conversions on her website. Mary can use this ad to bring warm prospects to her ecommerce store with the aim of getting them to purchase. (*Warmer audiences are more likely to convert.*)

The overall aim with cold audiences is to introduce your brand to them and then warm them up.

Chapter 6

CASE STUDIES: IRISH ORGANISATIONS USING FACEBOOK

6.1 CHARLENE FLANAGAN MAKEUP

Charlene Flanagan launched her makeup artistry business in 2014. From an early age Charlene had an interest in makeup. Her mother is a professional beauty therapist and she encouraged Charlene by teaching her all there was to know about makeup application. As Charlene grew older her passion for makeup intensified and in 2013 she successfully completed an International Diploma in Makeup Artistry.

6.1.1 GROWING THE FIRST 3,000 LIKES

Charlene said that when she started out makeup was just a hobby. Initially Facebook was the only social network she used. 'It can be disheartening when you start off, but my advice is to stick with it. Work hard, post consistently and learn from what's working on your page.'

Charlene said that the first group of people who liked and shared her content was her friends and family. 'The people closest to you will always be your first supporters. It's really important to call on them when you're starting out. Ask people to like your page and recommend it to their friends. Ask them to like and share your content. They will be your first brand ambassadors.' Charlene recognised this and used it to her advantage. But more importantly, she also realised that good quality content had the potential to draw in new fans who didn't know her.

She identified that there was a big appetite among women in their twenties and thirties for makeup tips and advice. 'No one was really pushing out that type of content at the time.' Charlene started doing 'before and after' looks with makeup. She found that this type of content went down really well with her fans. From there Charlene started sharing makeup application tips. 'At the time no one else locally was publishing this type of content. There was almost a shroud of secrecy around giving makeup tips.' Charlene's fans liked this type of content so much they shared it with their friends. 'Before I knew it, I had 3,000 fans and that gave me the motivation to grow it even more.'

Initially Charlene's audience was predominantly local people. She recognised that if she created content that her fans liked it helped the page likes to grow. 'I remember when I hit 5,000 likes, I thought it couldn't get much bigger…. But then it did.'

6.1.2 FROM 5,000 TO 20,000 FANS

As her business started to take off, Charlene was mindful of tuning into her customers' needs. 'I took note of common questions customers asked me and from this came up with content ideas for my Facebook page.'

On the following page is an example of a post Charlene created in response to a common question asked by customers. This is the type of content that fans like, comment and share – because they find it useful. I like this post because it's obvious from the first sentence what the post is about and Charlene has used an image to further emphasise the subject of the post. This advice is 'evergreen' and can be used again in the future. (Fig. 6.1)

Fig. 6.1

Charlene uses native video content regularly on her page and remembers with fondness the first video she published. 'I was really nervous about doing my first video. I did a five minute makeup tutorial and uploaded it directly from my phone with no editing one evening. Within four hours the video had 20,000 views and over 300 comments. I couldn't believe it the next morning when the video had 30,000 views and had even been shared by a Perth-based blogger.'

After that Charlene started using video more and more regularly. 'I invested in a good phone that produced video in HD. When I'm recording videos I use good lighting and choose backgrounds that don't distract. I tend not to edit the videos as raw video look more real.'

Charlene uses Facebook Live regularly on her page. 'I love Facebook Live, I love the way Facebook notifies my fans that I'm broadcasting. This really helps with audience figures.'

Facebook Live broadcasts appear higher in the news feed when they are live. After that they appear as videos on Charlene's page. In the live broadcast below you can see that the post reached 57,000 people, there were just under 15,000 views and there were 214 peak live viewers. (Fig. 6.2)

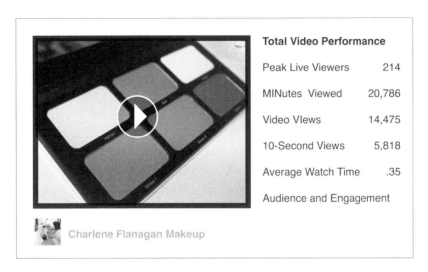

Total Video Performance

Peak Live Viewers	214
MINutes Viewed	20,786
Video VIews	14,475
10-Second Views	5,818
Average Watch Time	.35
Audience and Engagement	

Charlene Flanagan Makeup

Fig. 6.2

Charlene now has over 20,000 fans on her Facebook page. She puts her success on Facebook down to the following factors:

- A focus on producing great content that appeals to her fans
- Being one of the first to talk about new products, new techniques and in general being on top of her game. This means tuning into what's happening in her industry and acting quickly when announcements come through.
- Putting a lot of time and effort into social media. Time to come up with content and time to produce posts that have the best chance of performing well organically.
- Allocating budget for Facebook ads to grow page likes, boost posts and promote events on Eventbrite.

6.1.3 OTHER SOCIAL NETWORKS

Charlene currently uses a combination of social networks as part of her marketing communications strategy. Snapchat enables

Charlene to reach followers all over the world. She finds Instagram and Twitter useful for reaching out to brands. Facebook is the most important channel because it not only enables Charlene to reach customers and potential customers, it also is the platform which delivers the most in terms of sales.

6.1.4 WHAT ADVICE WOULD YOU GIVE TO OTHERS STARTING A FACEBOOK PAGE?

Charlene advises anyone starting out to work hard, stick at it, focus on producing great content, use video and Facebook Live and have a budget set aside for Facebook Ads.

6.2 DISCOVER ENNISCRONE

Discover Enniscrone is a community-run, not-for-profit group. Its aim is to promote Enniscrone as a holiday destination. The committee is run by volunteers who give their time freely for the benefit of the local community. Its Facebook page has been up and running since 2012 and has over 18,000 likes.

In 2013 a new visual identify was developed for Discover Enniscrone. The new logo is rectangular in shape and works really well on www.DiscoverEnniscrone.com.

As social media profile pictures are generally square or round, rectangular-shaped logos tend to be ill fitting. By the time the rectangular-shaped logo is sized down to fit the square or round shape it can appear too small. It's important to choose a profile picture carefully as it not only appears on your page, it is also the thumbnail that represents your page in the news feed. For this reason a square version of the logo was developed specifically for use on social media. The square logo sits really well in the profile picture and also is easily recognisable as a thumbnail in the news feed. (Fig. 6.3)

Fig. 6.3

Where possible cover images should use brand colours. Here is an example of a cover image. As you can see it uses many images, selected to appeal to the target markets and the brand colours are integrated subtly in the image. (Fig. 6.4)

Fig. 6.4

The call to action button on the page is to watch their promotional video. This creates a link to a YouTube video that the group had developed in 2013.

All seven members of the Discover Enniscrone Committee are administrators of the page. As the page is run by volunteers it's important that the work load is shared between many people. They have established 'page posting guidelines' to ensure consistency with the brand voice and that high organic reach of the page is maintained.

1. Always use images/video (i.e not a text-only post) and where possible integrate the Discover Enniscrone logo and/or brand colours. This is important as posts with images/videos that are relevant and appeal to the target audience are more likely to perform well in the news feed.

2. Always include a description with images/videos to encourage post engagement. Posting an image or a video without telling your audience why you are sharing it or why it should be of interest will limit its reach. Spending a few extra minutes thinking about your target audience and what you can say to encourage them to click on multiple images or watch a video or engage (react, comment or share) will promote a higher organic reach.

3. Create posts for the page rather than always sharing from other pages to maximise the number of people who see the post. Sharing posts from other pages can be a quick way to create a post for a page, but the organic reach of such posts is always lower than for a new post created from scratch. If the original post was sharing a link to a webpage, simply recreate the new post by sharing the same link, tag the page that published the original post and use the same image they used. This also applies to event pages created by other business pages.

4. Tag other pages where possible. Make other pages aware that you are talking about them by tagging them. Tag businesses that are being mentioned in the post.

5. Keep all posts at least five hours apart. If posts are published too close together the organic reach of the second and subsequent posts decreases. Unless you have really compelling content, my advice is keep posts at least five hours apart. If you have multiple administrators on a page, before you post check that no one else has posted in the last few hours. It's also worth checking to see if any posts are scheduled to

be published. If you find that a post has been (or is about to be) published, schedule your post to be published at a later time or even perhaps the next day. In this way both posts will have maximum opportunity to perform well in the news feed and you won't upset your page likes by clogging up their news feeds. Another option is to reschedule a scheduled post to enable you to publish newsworthy posts. Of course there are exceptions to this rule! If you are publishing content about a major news story and your fans are watching your page for updates, then by all means post updates as needed. Monitor the organic reach and the engagement levels of each post. If the organic reach starts to reduce, then pull back on the number of posts you are publishing.

The committee also set up a private group for all committee members. This is a very useful way to communicate about committee issues as well as what's happening on the Facebook page.

The success of any page will be directly related to the quality of content published. Good content that is of interest to its target audience will perform well in the news feed.

The goal of their posts is to:

- Promote subscribers to discover Enniscrone
- Promote events taking place in the town and in neighbouring towns
- Communicate news items
- Communicate the unique selling propositions of Enniscrone as a holiday destination
- Drive traffic back to the Discover Enniscrone website
- Promote any blogs published on the Discover Enniscrone website.

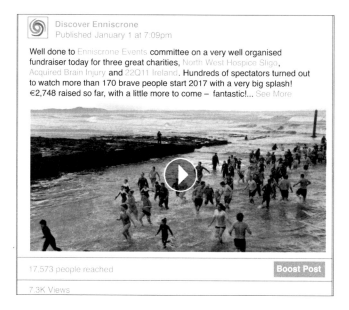

Fig. 6.5

The post shown in Fig. 6.5 performed well with an organic reach of 17,573 and 7,300 video views. Here are the reasons why it did so well:

- The timing of the post was good. It was posted four hours after the event took place. If the post had been published the following day it would have been old news. Posting in the evening time works well as engagement levels for this page tend to be higher at this time.

- It's a video. We know that video posts receive up to 300 per cent more reach in the news feed than a text-only post. The video was recorded using a smart phone and it's just over one minute in duration.

- The event organisers' 'Enniscrone Events' page has been tagged. Other pages tagged are the charities that benefited from the event – North West Hospice Sligo, Acquiried Brain Injury Ireland and 22Q11 Ireland. Tagging other pages lets them know you are 'talking' about them. There's a high likelihood that they may share on the post, especially a post with a video from the event. (Fig. 6.6)

Fig. 6.6

- The description of the post is insightful. The tone of the post description is enthusiastic, optimistic and infectious! Also, if someone views this post in their news feed they will have to click the 'see more' to read the complete text. When people click on posts to 'see more', it also counts as an engagement in the form of a click.

- By clicking on the link shown in blue below '17,573 people reached', a detailed analysis on how the post performed appears. (Fig. 6.7)

- This post was seen by 17,573 people and there were 7,338 video views of three seconds or more. If you click on the video views, you can get more information on the length of time people watched. People who watch the video for even just 10 seconds will have higher brand recall. A total of 349 people reacted to the post with 336 likes, 8 loves, 4 wows and 1 sad. There were 45 comments and 31 shares. Facebook also gives a breakdown of where the reactions, comments and shares were on the post itself or on shares (when someone shares the post in their news feed and people react, comment or share it from there).

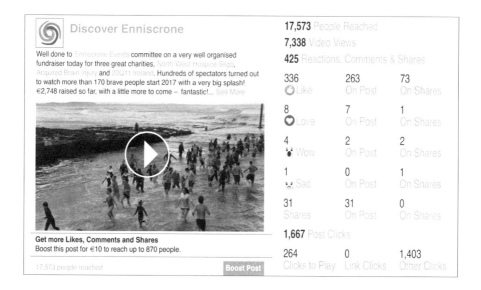

Fig. 6.7

Fig. 6.8

The post shown in Fig. 6.8 is an example of supporting one of the businesses that subscribe to Discover Enniscrone. As you can see from the post, rather than sharing a post from Gilroy's page, a post was created using the event image which was downloaded from Gilroy's page.

Gilroy's Bar is tagged in the post letting administrators know that a post about them has been created on the Discover Enniscrone Facebook page. It also makes it easy for fans of Discover Enniscrone to click through to Gilroy Bar's page as the tag is a direct link to it. The bands playing at the celebration are also tagged in this post. As you can see from the 'shares' on the post, members of the bands tagged shared the post in their news feeds. (Fig. 6.9)

Fig. 6.9

The post achieved good organic reach appearing in the newsfeed of 3,477 people. There were 62 reactions, comments and shares. (Fig. 6.10)

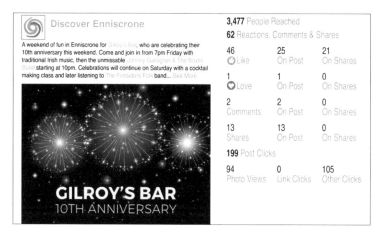

Fig. 6.10

The post shown in Fig. 6.11 is another example of a post which promotes the subscribers of this marketing committee. In this example seven images were uploaded of different outdoor family activities in Enniscrone. These images were then used to create a slide show thus creating a 14 second video. As you can see in the post, the proposition is a family day out and activity providers in Enniscrone are tagged in the image. Tagged businesses and other local organisations shared the post which meant it was seen by many more people. It's a great example of businesses working with each other to promote Enniscrone as a destination.

This post reached 12,697 people. There were high engagement levels with 167 reactions, 5 comments and 33 shares.

Posts with seascape images as shown in Fig. 6.12, combined with a call to action to make a trip to Enniscrone, work well on this page. Fans love this type of post which is reflected in the post engagement levels. It's important to get the timing right, tag other relevant pages that might share and include a post description that includes a call to action while also encouraging post engagement.

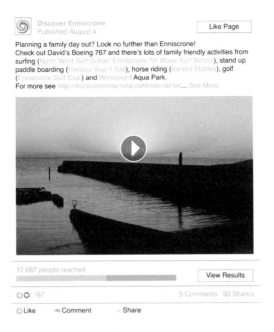

Fig. 6.11

Fig. 6.12

Below is a panoramic image which is an interactive photo. Facebook prompts users to hold their phones up and move them around to view different parts of the photo. The post reached over 12,000 people and achieved high levels of engagement with 250 reactions, 11 comments and 34 shares. (Fig. 6.13)

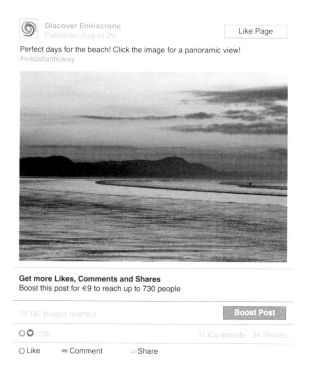

Fig. 6.13

Local businessman David McGowan made headlines around the world when he transported a Boeing 767 airplane from Shannon up the West Coast of Ireland by sea, and landed it on Enniscrone beach. The plane is the centrepiece of a transport-themed glamping village in Enniscrone. Such was the media interest in the story that a national radio station broadcast live from Enniscrone beach the day the plane was beached. The story made international headlines and created a social media frenzy. It was a unique opportunity for the Discover Enniscrone committee to bring their brand to a worldwide audience and to work with

David McGowan and his team at Quirky Nights Glamping Village to broadcast updates on the move as it was happening. From April 28 to May 17 there were 53 posts on the page. The committee worked closely with David McGowan and his team to bring many exclusive updates on the project. The combined reach of those posts was an astounding 1,000,273 and the page likes grew from 6,000 to 12,000.

This was the most successful post with a reach of 259,152. It's a collage of images, some captured by committee members, some shared with the page by members of the public. The post was published the morning after the plane was successfully installed at the Quirky Glamping Nights site. The fact that seven images were posted meant that people had to click the images to see all seven. The engagement on the post was extremely high with 9,769 reactions, comments and shares. There were 67,782 post clicks, 36,118 of which were photo views. (Fig. 6.14)

Fig. 6.14

6.3 MORANS BUTCHERS AND DELI

Kevin Moran opened his traditional butchers and deli in Ballina, County Mayo in 1985. Kevin believes that the way small retailers have marketed themselves has changed considerably over the years. He remembers a time when he was a child and shop owners could simply put a sign in their window to attract customers. 'It was a level playing field in terms of marketing back then.' Before Kevin opened his business he worked as a butcher in Quinnsworth. He can remember it being a big deal when the company took out radio adverts on the national airwaves. Nowadays it's hard to avoid aggressive advertising from large multinationals on TV, radio and newspapers. Kevin believes it's hard for small independent retailers to compete as they don't have the same resources to get their message to potential customers. He has long felt that competing with large supermarkets that are aggressively targeting the fresh food market has been a challenge for butchers everywhere.

He believes that Facebook is a game changer for small businesses. Kevin describes Facebook as a 'powerful yet cost effective tool that enables him to reach customers within a 50 kilometre radius of his shop'.

6.3.1 FACEBOOK MARKETING BOOTCAMP

I started working with Kevin during the summer of 2016. Kevin had been using Facebook for a few years but felt he needed to be more strategic about his efforts.

Kevin joined my ten-week Facebook Marketing programme. Each week we dealt with one aspect of Facebook marketing so it was never too much to take in at the one time. Each week I sent Kevin a video tutorial and a number of tasks to complete that related to it. He also had to post two to three times every week on his page. We had weekly Skype calls to review progress, discuss issues and plan the week ahead.

The ten weeks of the programme covered the following topics:

- Review of page setup
- Setting short and medium term SMART Goals
- Review brand assets
- Customer analysis and profiling
- Content planning and creation
- Using videos/Facebook Live
- Facebook Insights – analysing what's working
- Facebook ads.

As Kevin is a local business, reaching people near his premises and differentiating himself from his competitors were high priorities for him.

As part of the course Kevin undertook some primary market research. He interviewed a number of customers, had brainstorming sessions with staff and carried out a customer survey. From this Kevin was able to create a number of customer personas representing his different target audiences.

Creating the personas helped Kevin to come up with content that they would find interesting, useful and that would position Kevin as an expert.

Through watching the tutorials and by posting regularly Kevin began to improve the quality of the posts on his page by:

- Investing time to research competing content
- Using media rich content – sourcing and resizing images as well as creating branded images using tools like Canva.
- Tagging other pages where possible
- Encouraging engagement on the post

- Being mindful of when his posts were published to maximise organic reach.

Below is a post that Kevin published on his page which I really like. Kevin created the image for the post using the online photo imaging tool, Canva. I like the way he has integrated the company logo and brand colours. He has also kept the image text to a minimum. In his post description he aims to get the reader's attention in the first few words. He has also integrated some good advice on what to serve with the steaks. People are more likely to engage with a post, even tag friends or share it on their news feed, if they find the information in the post useful.

As you can see from the insights below, the post performed really well organically reaching just under 2,000 people (over double the number who liked his page at the time). Kevin then boosted the post to people living in his catchment area and spent a further €10 reaching an additional 2,200 people.

The engagement levels on the post were really good with 92 reactions, comments and shares. There were 170 posts clicks. The people who engaged with this post are also more likely to see posts from this page in the future. (Fig. 6.15)

Fig. 6.15

This is an example of Kevin positioning himself as an expert and offering useful advice to his customers. He recorded the video himself using his smart phone and kept it under one minute. The post description is good, capturing the attention of the reader immediately. It gives the viewer some idea of what's in the video. The content is 'evergreen', meaning that Kevin can use the video again for future posts as the advice will never date.

The post reached 1,374 people with 707 video views. Engagement levels on the post were high too with 45 reactions, comments and shares. (Fig. 6.16)

Fig. 6.16

On the following page is an example of encouraging customers to connect with staff. One of Kevin's team, Ray, who has been working with Kevin for over 10 years, was turning 40. As noted previously, people want to connect and do business with people. Customers knew Ray from coming into the store and were happy to engage with the post to convey their birthday wishes. The post reached 3,108 people which is 200 per cent of the page likes. It attracted 153 reactions, comments and shares. (Fig. 6.17)

Post Details Reported stats may be delayed from what appears on posts.

Morans Butchers and Deli
Published October 22

He will be 40 tomorrow and he's proud of it! Best wishes Ray from your colleagues and friends on reaching this significant milestone

3,108 People Reached
153 Reactions, Comments & Shares

120 Like	88 On Post	32 On Shares
3 Love	70 On Post	3 On Shares
3 Haha	1 On Post	2 On Shares
24 Comment	19 On Post	5 On Shares
3 Shares	1 On Post	2 On Shares

343 Post Clicks

100 Photo Views	0 Link Clicks	243 Other Clicks

NEGATIVE FEEDBACK
0 Hide Post   0 Hide All Posts
0 Report as Spam   0 Unlike Page

Get more Likes, Comments and Shares
Boost this post for €19 to reach up to 7,700 people.

3,108 people reached   Boost Post

89   19 Comments 1 Share

Fig. 6.17

The post on the following page is a good example of Kevin tapping into what was happening in the town and county at the time. The Mayo GAA Senior Team was playing in the All Ireland Final. The post was published two days before the final when excitement around the county was hitting fever pitch. The post cleverly integrates products from around the county, thus further tapping into the 'pride in the county' mood. I like the way the image integrates the brand colours and logo.

The post reached 2,577 people with 54 reactions, comments and shares. (Fig. 6.18)

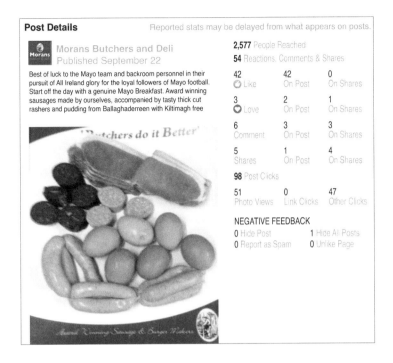

Fig. 6.18

6.3.2 USE OF FACEBOOK ADS

Kevin believes that traditional butchers all over Ireland have lost market share in response to marketing tactics by the major supermarkets that have the budget to use TV, radio and national print media to reach their target audience. Kevin feels that Facebook ads are a game changer as they give small businesses like his the opportunity to reach a local audience for as little as €1.00.

6.4 GUNA NUA BOUTIQUE

Suzanne Kilkenny is the founder of Guna Nua Boutique. Suzanne has two shops in Ballina and Westport in County Mayo, and has recently launched an online store, www.GunaNuaBoutique.ie.

Suzanne, a Galway native, saw a gap in the market in Ballina for a women's boutique in 2011. Suzanne has years of experience in retail having worked in the sector since she was 16. Her introduction to trading online was selling baby wear on eBay whilst on maternity leave. It was then that Suzanne realized the importance of visual merchandising online and she spent time setting up and taking high quality images. Suzanne could see that the quality of images had a direct impact on sales. This experience became apparent when it came to setting up and managing the Guna Nua Boutique Facebook page.

Suzanne says that in her opinion, Facebook is one of the best free marketing tools for showcasing her business and generating sales. The Guna Nua Boutique Facebook page has over 72,000 fans. Suzanne has grown her fan base through hard work and perseverance. It has helped Suzanne grow her business by raising brand awareness and bringing people into her stores. It also generated online sales with customers all over the world. Sales came though the Facebook page in the form of private messages, phone calls, and emails. Suzanne's business was one of the few in Ireland that had a booming online business, even though she didn't launch Guna Nua Boutique ecommerce store until November 2016.

The success of her Facebook page can be attributed to the following factors.

Hard Work

Suzanne has always worked hard on her page. She spends time researching great content. By monitoring how posts perform, she has learned which ones appeal to her audience, and works consistently to publish the right kind of content on her page.

She Never Forgets Her Customers

From dealing with customers in her stores, Suzanne knows the type of advice they value. She understands that people appreciate advice on matching outfits with shoes, jewellery and other accessories. She uses this to create posts which replicate this guidance. If her recommendations are relevant and appreciated by customers in her stores, it will be equally well-received by her Facebook audience. Using this formula for creating posts has worked for Suzanne time and time again. (Fig. 6.19)

Fig. 6.19

On the following page is another great example from the Guna Nua Boutique page. (Fig. 6.20)

going...going...almost gone!
20% OFF EVERYTHING #online ENDS TOMORROW!
http://www.gunanuaboutique.ie/p.little.mistress-n.../p-4280c4b...
See More...

Fig. 6.20

Good Quality Images

Suzanne has always used high quality images on her page. She sources images from suppliers and from other social media networks. Sometimes she'll even use images that look closely like items from her store. She covers herself by using terms like 'inspired by' and 'shop the look'. This is clever and it means that the images on her page always look professional. (Fig. 6.20)

Tuned In

Suzanne tunes into what celebrities at home and abroad are wearing. Posting images of celebrities wearing items she sells in the shop leads to instant sales. If Suzanne spots a celebrity wearing an item from her store, she posts an image on her page as soon as she can. She uses the app PicCollage to create a collage of images of the celebrity and the item of clothing from her store.

Fig. 6.21

One evening Suzanne spotted a photo of Kate Middleton wearing a dress very similar to one in her store and on her ecommerce site. Using PicCollage she posted an image of the dress she had for sale alongside Kate with the caption '#Stealherstyle' and a link to where the dress could be purchased on her ecommerce store. Within twenty seconds there was a sale of the dress on her ecommerce store. There were so many sales of that dress throughout the evening and night that Suzanne had to start work at 5.00 am the following morning to organise deliveries.

Suzanne also works with micro-influencers locally. She finds that when she works with local beauty bloggers it has an impact of sales in her Mayo-based stores.

What's in the News

Suzanne regularly posts about what's in the news if she believes it will be of interest to her fans. These types of posts tend to perform well and they make her page interesting. I love the post below featuring the popular hashtag #COYBIG (Come on You Boys in Green). The Irish soccer team, rugby team and Conor McGregor all won various fixtures over the course of one weekend and the mood was high across the country. This is a great example of appealing to your audience. This post had 119 reactions and 23 shares. Fab! (Fig. 6.22)

Fig. 6.22

Mix It Up

Suzanne recognises that using memes that appeal to her audience keep engagement levels high. This assists the organic reach of her page. When people engage (click, react, comment, share) her posts, they are more likely to see future posts from the page. She has a few favourite memes that she uses on the page when she feels it needs a lift. She reckons that if the memes still makes her laugh, then her fans will enjoy them too. Below is an example of one of Suzanne's favorites. As you can see from the image it had a reach of 26,412 people, with 287 reactions, 10 comments and 25 shares. (Fig. 6.23)

Gúna Nua Boutique
November 5

#fact!!

No matter how big and bad you
are, when a two year old hands
you a toy phone, you answer it!

Like   Comment   Share

287   25 shares

Fig. 6.23

Tagging

Suzanne uses tagging effectively to reach out to fashion bloggers and other influential social media accounts. This, too, has the impact of maintaining high levels of organic reach. When people are tagged, they sometimes share the post with their fans.

Committed

Suzanne takes time to respond to all comments and messages on the page. When she opened her first shop in Ballina, she said she would work all day in the shop and then spend up to three hours every evening working on her page. Responding to people personally makes them feel valued, and helps grow brand loyalty.

Competitions

Suzanne picked up 5,000 fans in one week through running a competition to give away two One Direction tickets. Suzanne knew this would appeal to the mothers of One Direction fans, who were her audience. The winner of the competition was so delighted that she sent on videos from the concert, which made for great content for Suzanne's Facebook page.

Getting to over 70,000 fans did not happen by accident. Suzanne works hard, is tuned into the media, what's happening in the world, and which celebrities are wearing her brands. The important thing is that, although it involves work and commitment, she enjoys it and it ultimately leads to sales. After all, isn't that what it's all about?

6.5 WATERPOINT

Waterpoint is a community-run, not-for-profit organisation. Facilities include an indoor heated pool with flume waterslide, kiddies pool, indoor children's play room and a state of the art gym.

Using Facebook is an important part of Waterpoint's marketing strategy. During the holiday season Waterpoint uses its Facebook page to encourage people holidaying in the area to visit the facility. It also targets families living within a one hour radius for day trips. During the off season the focus is on children's swimming lessons, birthday parties and gym membership.

In 2015 Waterpoint carried out a review of its visual identity. The company had been using a logo which had been developed when the facility opened in the 1990s. Management at Waterpoint did not have a high resolution version of the logo and this was an issue every time the logo needed to be used on marketing collateral such as brochures, pull up stands, road signs and print ads. (Fig. 6.24)

Fig. 6.24

A local graphic designer, Barry Jordan of Spear Design, was employed to update the logo. The new logo used elements of the original, including the building and the sunset theme, and also incorporated graphics representing the waterslide as well as a splash effect. The shape, colours and font give it a modern feel and Barry supplied Waterpoint with high resolution versions for print and low resolution images for digital use. The main logo is rectangular and works well in the company website (see Fig 6.25). A stacked or square version was also developed for use on social media channels. (Fig. 6.26)

Fig. 6.25

The square version of the logo works well as the profile picture on the Waterpoint Facebook page. The stacked or square shape sits pefectly into the square-shaped profile image and the image fills the entire space. It's easily identifiable both in the profile image and as a thumbnail. It's important that the image is distinguishable as a thumbnail as this is what most people see in their news feeds. (Fig. 6.27)

Fig. 6.26

Calling all members new and old!
We want to help you achieve your goals.
We are running a 6 week challenge programme exclusively for our members!
See More...

Fig. 6.27

Barry Jordan supplied the colour references for the brand palate making it easier for staff to use them consistently across all online and offline marketing activities. (Fig. 6.28)

Fig. 6.28

Waterpoint uses Facebook effectively to reach its customers. The following image is quite good from a branding perspective. This image was created in Canva and uses the brand colours. Text on the image is kept to a minimum to keep it under 20 per cent.

At the time the post was published Facebook would not approve adds containing images with over 20 per cent text. Although it has relaxed on this rule, it is still advisable to keep text to a minimum as it impacts on the reach and cost of the ads. Ads with images with over 20 per cent text tend to cost more.

When images like this, incorporating brand colours, are published on a page it makes it look more professional and reinforces your brand identify (Figs. 6.29 and 6.30). As you can see from the image below, Waterpoint's branding is very strong on their Facebook page with their logo as the profile picture and their brand colours used effectively in their cover image. (Fig. 6.29)

Fig. 6.29

Fig. 6.30

6.5.1 POSTING STRATEGY

Waterpoint uses its Facebook page regularly to get its brand in front of potential customers. Its posting strategy is to:

- Post about products and services
- Posts tips and advice that customers will find useful
- Enable customers to connect with staff
- Have some fun.

Below is a great example of a fun post. A member of staff found a child's doll that had been left behind after a family visit. A simple image caption was printed and photographed with the doll. This was then used to create a Facebook post.

The post reached 10,293 people, more than three times the number of people who liked that page at the time. It had 360 reactions, comments and shares. The post was shared by 166 people. All this exposure for the cost of some quick thinking and clever posting. (Fig. 6.31)

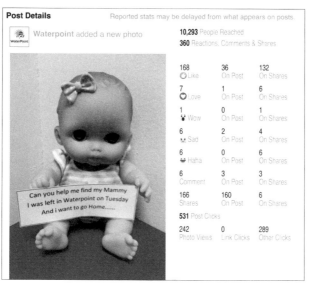

Fig. 6.31

As noted previously, people are more likely to engage with posts if they find the information useful. Instead of being concerned with 'what you have to say about your products and services', by offering advice that the reader finds useful you position yourself as an expert and encourage your customers to trust you. This post is an example of offering some advice to members who are weight conscious. Remember, *it's not about what you want to say, it's about what your customers want to hear.* (Fig. 6.32)

Fig. 6.32

Facebook is a powerful marketing tool that enables you to get your brand in front of people who are most likely to buy from you. The post on the following page was published shortly after a new gym was installed. I like how the post incorporates 16 images. Anyone interested in the gym who wants to see all images has to click on them. These 'clicks' are counted as post engagements. Facebook's news feed algorithm monitors interactions such as this. When a post achieves high engagements, Facebook is more likely to show it to more of the page's fans. This post reached 7,080 people, over twice as many than liked the Facebook page at the time. This was because 31 people shared the post in their news feed, thus exposing the post to their friends who might not previously have been fans of the Waterpoint page. (Fig. 6.33)

Fig. 6.33

It's important to let your fans connect with you and your staff on your Facebook page. Posts that feature your staff celebrating a big life event (wedding, birthday, promotion etc.) tend to perform well in the news feed as your page fans are more likely to engage with them. And your brand will benefit because you are reminding your customers that you exist. Again, you don't have to be selling in every post to do this.

When a member of staff came across a scrapbook of old photos of Waterpoint down through the years, she used her phone to take photos of these images. She then used Pages Manager on her smart phone to create a post. As the post had over 20 images, anyone interested had to click through to see them. All clicks count as post engagements.

The reaction to the post was amazing with people looking through the images and tagging friends who featured. Not only did the post get the Waterpoint brand in front of potential customers, it also reminded people that Waterpoint is a community-run, not-for-profit organisation that benefits people locally. (Fig. 6.34)

Fig. 6.34

6.6 LIMERICK STRAND HOTEL

The four star Limerick Strand Hotel is located on the banks of the river Shannon in the heart of Limerick city. Hotel management recognised the importance of social media in the early 2000s when brands in Ireland started integrating digital platforms into their marketing strategies. Since then a senior member of the hotel's marketing team has been growing its reputation online.

I spoke with Claireann McKeon, who manages the hotel's social media. Social media is an important part of the hotel's digital marketing strategy. They use several platforms including Facebook, Instagram, Twitter and Pinterest. The social media plan is integrated into the annual sales, marketing and PR plan.

The hotel's page started off as a 'friend page' as that's all that was available at the time. The hotel converted it to a fan page when Facebook introduced business pages, and since then has grown its fan base to 23,000. Organic growth was easier at the start. Facebook is now a much busier platform and while organic growth is still possible, it's more difficult.

Last year hotel management offered guests the option to log on to the hotel's WiFi by liking its Facebook page. This generated 5,500 Facebook page likes and facilitated remarketing to these guests through Facebook organic reach and Facebook ads.

6.6.1 KNOWING YOUR CUSTOMERS

Claireann believes that social media is about building relationships with customers and having conversations with them. She knows the profile of customers who connect with the hotel using social media. They tend to be female, are aged between 24 and 34 and live within a 30 kilometre radius of the hotel. Google analytics statistics from the hotel's website traffic shows a similar profile.

Identifying to whom you are talking is a vital part of any conversation. It affects the content, tone, language, timing and proposition.

The hotel uses its social media channels to drive wedding bookings. According to Claireann the hotel actively targets females aged between 24 and 34 who have recently changed their Facebook relationship status to 'getting married'. She said it also targets females up to 65 as often the initial phone call comes from the bride's mother. Some brides might not be living locally but are coming home to get married.

The hotel uses Facebook to reach a local audience for ground floor business in the bar and restaurant. The hotel's head chef, Tom Flavin, has his own following on social media so this facilitates reaching out to 'foodies'. Claireann says that Tom understands how social media works and how important it is to the business.

He features regularly in their social media posts. Posts with a 'hard sell' don't work so instead they push out content like Tom working in the kitchen or featuring the restaurant and bar staff. A video of Vicki, the restaurant manager, giving a video tour of the Sunday buffet had 8,625 organic (non-paid for) views in two days. While it's important to get professional videos of the hotel, Claireann says the videos they record themselves perform better as they look more authentic. People love authentic content. (Fig. 6.35)

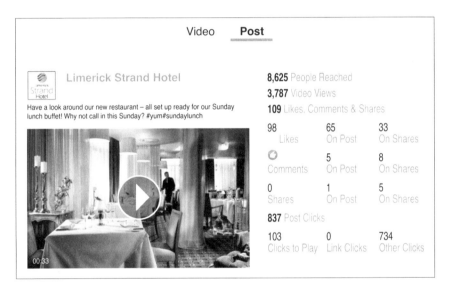

Fig. 6.35

6.6.2 CONTENT CALENDAR

Generating good content takes planning, experience and time. Claireann prepares an annual content calendar. This enables her to plan content for the year in advance. At a top level, content planning is done around key dates like St Patrick's Day, Easter, Father's Day, Christmas, New Year, Valentine's Day, Mother's Day, etc. At the start of each quarter more detailed planning takes place, and again at the beginning of each month. This ensures a constant supply of quality content geared towards the hotel's target audiences.

Businesses that plan their content calendars in this way tend to be more successful on Facebook and across other social media platforms because they give themselves time to be creative and to consider what will resonate with their audiences.

Updates on the hotel's Facebook page are limited to one post a day – Claireann is mindful not to bombard people with too many posts. Eighty per cent of posts are hotel-related and 20 per cent are what's happening in the Limerick, the wider region and the Wild Atlantic Way.

Three to five posts are scheduled a week on the Facebook page leaving room to react to news items and user-generated content.

The management team understands how important it is to react to what's happening in the hotel, the city and anything or anyone linked to the hotel. They monitor closely what's being said about the hotel and respond quickly.

All hotel employees are made aware of the importance of reacting quickly to anything out of the ordinary. An employee 'WhatsApp' group ensures this timely response. Images, videos and updates are shared in the group and social media administrators curate this content across all of the hotel's social media networks. Claireann is careful about what she posts on her Facebook page. She said that the hotel team is committed; they share out the page's content all the time which significantly improves its organic reach.

6.6.3 WORKING WITH INFLUENCERS

The hotels uses a tool called Revinate to alert the team when high influencers check in to the hotel. While all guests are valued and treated with the highest levels of customer service, influencers with a significant social media following are sometimes sent an extra treat. Something as simple as a basket of homemade cookies can inspire guests to share their delight across their social media platforms.

Getting endorsements from influencers like bloggers and celebrities is an effective way of growing brand awareness, increasing followers on social media and bringing paying customers through the door. Claireann gives the example of a post where Pippa O'Connor shared an image from the hotel's presidential suite which was liked by 5,500 people! People like to associate themselves with celebrities and it's important to take advantage of content generated by influencers.

The hotel is closely aligned with Munster rugby, and works with some of the players who act as brand ambassadors for the hotel. When it shares their images it always generates high engagement levels across all social media platforms.

A key element of the hotel's social media strategy is to publish user-generated content. They find that their followers react more to images taken by guests rather than professional images. They could spend €5,000 on a photo shoot and find their followers react more to an amateur photo taken by a guest. User-generated content is considered to be more authentic and therefore more like a third party endorsement.

6.6.5 MEDIA-RICH CONTENT

Clarieann recommends using Canva.com to design and resize images. At the hotel, they use a combination of their own, professional and stock images.

Claireann says that video is very important. The hotel recently employed Ktown Media to produce a fully immersed 360 degree video tour of the hotel for their Facebook page. The video provided viewers with a guided tour of the hotel and even invited people to look out over the edge of the rooftop! This post had a massive organic reach of over 12,000 people. (Fig. 6.36)

The hotel regularly broadcasts live from its Facebook page. This is particularly effective for cooking demonstrations. Head chef Tom Flavin features regularly in its Facebook Live broadcasts. These posts are a useful way of increasing brand awareness and generating food and beverage sales.

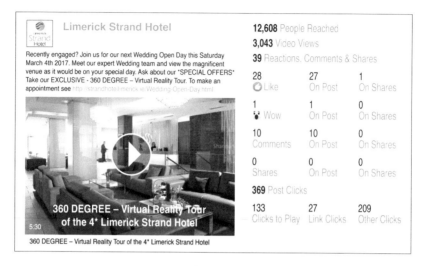

Fig. 6.36

Claireann recognises the importance of keeping up to date with current trends. Last year at a Christmas Party for 470 people the hotel did the Mannequin Challenge. This post had a massive reach as people in the room tagged friends and shared it. Claireann says, 'It's about thinking on your feet. It's easier to react when you know what will appeal to your target audience.' (Fig. 6.37)

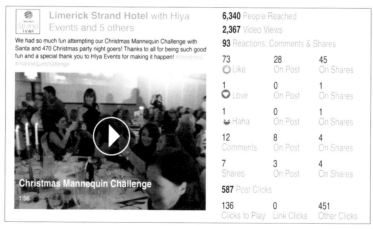

Fig. 6.37

The marketing team noticed that about six months ago bookings starting to come through Facebook Messenger. Claireann believes this trend emerged when Facebook added the 'responsive' feature to pages. She says it's a useful way of building rapport with customers and warming them to the brand.

The hotel has a budget of €100 per month for Facebook ads. It uses this to drive its wedding business. Claireann says that she also boosts posts with the aim of kickstarting organic shares.

6.6.6 ADVICE TO OTHERS

Claireann's advice to others:

- Get the basics right – telephone, phone number, address
- Keep it honest and real – show what's happening behind the scenes
- Remember where you are – your location
- Be a personality not a hotel – but be professional
- Introduce the staff – people love to meet the team
- Stay on trend but stay true to who you are – your brand
- Don't hide complaints – always answer them.
- Limit your time on social media – make it effective.
- Have a budget for Facebook ads – and experiment with it.

Claireann's role in the hotel is changing to reflect the time that is required to manage social media effectively. She is moving from a Sales and Marketing position to a Digital Marketing role. This reflects the importance of social media in the hotel's overall marketing strategy. 'Social media brings customers through the door – that's why we invest so much time and budget in it.'

6.7 BALLINROBE GAA

Liam Horan is the webmaster for Ballinrobe GAA Club and founder of www.localstreaming.club and Sli Nua Careers. Liam is a journalist and has worked for local and national media outlets including *The Irish Independent*, *Evening Echo*, RTÉ, *Athlone Voice*, Mid West Radio and *The Western People.*

It is not surprising to see Liam's media skills being put to good use on the Ballinrobe GAA social media channels and website.

The club is very aware of the different audiences it has visiting its page. It has parents of the Under 10 Bord Na nOg, ladies football players, senior club players and fans. The ladies have their own Facebook page but also feed into the main page through their PRO who is a page administrator.

Ballinrobe GAA Club is very active, particularly on Facebook. It is an integral part of their overall digital marketing strategy. According to Liam, when you're working with volunteers, it's important that tasks are carried out as efficiently as possible. For this reason, the club's social media channels are seamlessly integrated with their website. When articles are published on the website they are automatically shared across Facebook and Twitter. This takes the workload off volunteers and means that fans get news like match reports really fast. 'People don't want to wait for sports news anymore,' says Liam. Not many years ago, fans waited until the following day to hear the sports news but now, even at club level, they expect to hear it instantaneously.

6.7.1 THIRD PARTY APPS

Sport allows people to connect through shared moments. Social media keeps people connected with the club no matter where they are in the world.

Ballinarobe GAA has set up its social media so that a great deal can be done on the sideline at a match. Liam explains that it's too much hassle to go home and do it later and the audience wants the results right away. The audience accepts a rougher, less edited version of the report from the sideline if it means they don't have to wait for it.

The club uses the following apps to broadcast to fans worldwide.

Scoreboard App

The club uses a Scoreboard App called GAA Journo which publishes match score updates automatically to both the club's Facebook and Twitter accounts.

Spreaker

Liam speaks highly of another app, Spreaker, which enables match reports and commentaries to be broadcast live from the sideline. The free version of the app supports broadcasts of up to 29 minutes at a time, whereas the paid version ($150 per annum) supports up to 10 hours. The club initially used the free version and just stopped commentaries at about 27 minutes and then started a new podcast. Last year they upgraded and feel the investment was well worth it. It means that match reports are done when the final whistle sounds. This attracts listeners from all over the world when the broadcast is live and then a few hours later players and people who have attended the match can tune in.

LocalStreaming.Club

Localsteaming.club is a company founded by Liam Horan. It provides sporting organisations, community groups and businesses with the opportunity to broadcast live shows online either on social media or on their websites. It provides professional cameras, video and streaming technology, a commentator and, if necessary, a presenter. Live streams can be sponsored by the club or local businesses. It opens up the possibility to small sporting clubs to broadcast their games on the Internet to viewers all over the world. The use of professional cameras and a commentator is what differentiates this service from simply using a smart phone on the sideline.

According to Liam, 'anyone can stream, but it needs a journalist's or broadcaster's overview to be really effective and coherent'. Clubs need to think of what they're streaming, how they can stream it, how quirky it is and how integrated it is with their websites and other social media channels. Liam recommends that when it comes to prioritising and structuring a news item, club PROs need to use the 'inverted pyramid' approach where the article leads with the most newsworthy information to draw the audience in from the first sentence.

6.7.2 CONNECTING COMMUNITIES

Liam believes that sport offers people a sense of community and a sense of place. It creates the desire of wanting to belong to something. It unifies fans with a shared sense of longing at match defeats and elation following success. Liam says that sporting organisations need to see the smaller picture. The opportunity is to reach fans by broadcasting live with raw authentic content. It's social history in the making.

Globalisation is creating localisation by using social media to connect communities. Fans living away from home regularly get together to watch local matches. Some fans even come home from overseas for finals of local club competitions having followed all matches in that season online through social media and the club's website.

Ballinrobe vs Kilmeena Under 21 C Final 2016

Liam gave an example of a County Under 21 C final against Kilmeena. Commentators were Liam Horan, Padraic Costello, Tom Carney (Ballinrobe) and Micky Carney from Kilmeena. A full commentary of the match was broadcast along with a half an hour after the match in the Ballinrobe dressing room talking to players, parents and former players. Even though the broadcast is driven by Ballinrobe, it always invites contributors from the opposing clubs. More people tuned in to the broadcast than were at the match. A former player contacted Liam after that match to say he would be returning back to Ballinrobe from overseas as he had missed home so much the night they had won the final.

Ballinrobe Community School All Ireland Senior B Final 2017

Ballinrobe Community School won the All Ireland Senior B Title in Croke Park in 2017. Using Spreaker the Club broadcast a preview programme from Jury's Hotel featuring former players. The match was broadcast live on BallinrobeGaa.com and that night the homecoming, held in Ballinrobe, was broadcast on Facebook Live.

Ballinrobe Community School had previously won the title in 1990 and 1999. Two things were different about the 2017 win. Firstly, it was played in Croke Park, and secondly, it was broadcast, freely available, on Ballinrobe.com in audio, Mid West Radio in audio and TG4 Livestreaming video.

Mike Finnerty, a Sky Sports commentator and past pupil of Ballinrobe Community School, was overseas on holiday in Dubai. He tuned in live to all three platforms and later hosted a Ballinrobe party.

Chapter 7

FACEBOOK INSIGHTS

Facebook Insights provides statistical data on how your page is performing. It gives information on how many people are seeing your page, what their profile is and how they are engaging. You can use Facebook Insights to learn what's working on your page and what's not.

Facebook Insights is found on the admin panel at the top of your page. (Fig. 7.1)

Fig. 7.1

The insights section has an overview panel and a sub menu where all the statistics are broken in to different sections. (Fig. 7.2)

7.1 OVERVIEW

The overview section gives a snapshot of how your page has performed over the last seven days. You can quickly see:

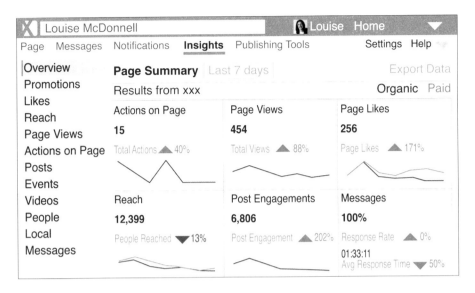

Fig. 7.2

- Actions on page – number of clicks on your page's contact info and call to action button

- Page views – number of times people viewed your page and its sections

- Page likes – number of new page likes

- Reach – number of people who saw any of your pages posts including paid and non-paid (organic)

- Post engagement – number of times people engaged with posts on your page (reactions, comments, shares, clicks)

- Messages – percentage of messages you have answered and your average response time

- Videos – number of times videos on your pages have been viewed for at least three seconds.

The overview page also has a summary of recent promotions (boosted posts) as well as a summary of how the last five posts on your page have performed.

Pages to Watch

See how your page performs compared to your competitors in this section. You can add up to five different pages to this section. Facebook will then rank all pages performance over the last week, including yours, with a breakdown by:

- Total pages likes
- Change in page likes
- Number of posts created
- Engagement levels.

Export Data

There is the facility to export data for a 90 day period to an excel sheet. You can export up to 500 posts at a time. This is useful when creating reports.

7.2 PROMOTIONS

A list of all the 'boosted posts' on your page. It gives a summary of the number of people reached, the number of engagements and the cost. (Fig. 7.3)

7.3 FOLLOWERS

Followers are people who have indicated to Facebook that they want to see your posts but do not want to be considered as a 'page like'. Fans can set how posts from a page they are following appear in their news feed. The current options are 'see first' and 'default'.

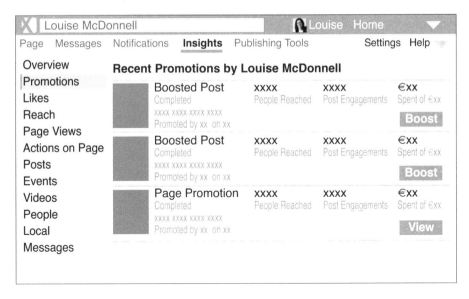

Fig. 7.3

Use this section (as with the 'likes' section below) to find out when people have followed and unfollowed your page and where on Facebook these actions took place (on your page, under page suggestions, ads etc.)

7.4 LIKES

In this section you can learn how your page likes are growing (page likes), the net likes (new likes minus unlikes) and where you are picking up the new page likes (on your page, page suggestions, desktop, ads, other).

You can set the date range at the top of this section which will give you a benchmark of how your page likes have grown over this period. In general, there is a strong correlation between posting good quality content that is relevant to your target audience and the increase of page likes. (Figs. 7.4, 7.5, 7.6)

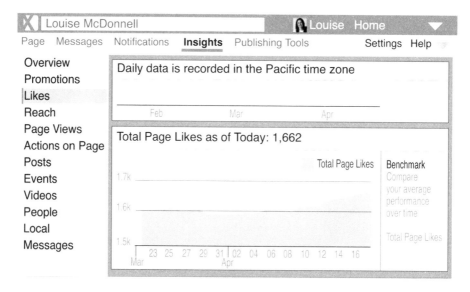

Fig. 7.4

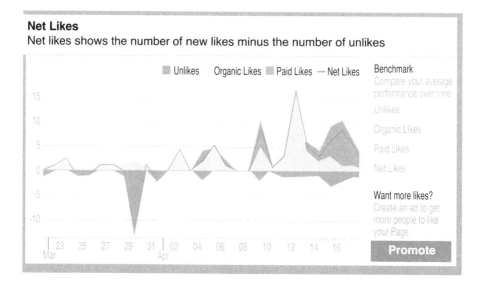

Fig. 7.5

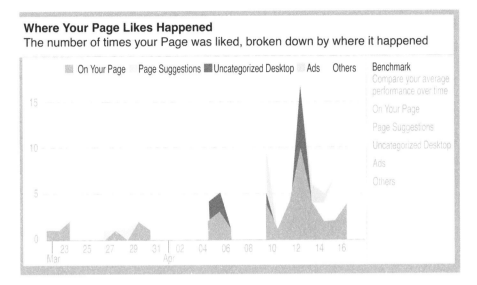

Where Your Page Likes Happened
The number of times your Page was liked, broken down by where it happened

Fig. 7.6

7.5 REACH

In this section you can learn about:

- Post reach: the number of people that saw your posts, with a breakdown of paid versus organic (non-paid).

- Reactions, comments, shares: The number of times people engaged with the posts on your page by reacting (like, love, ha ha, yay, wow, sad, angry), commenting or sharing.

- Reactions: A breakdown of reactions on posts (like, love, ha ha, yay, wow, sad, angry).

- Hide, report as spam and unlikes. A summary of the negative feedback on your pages posts.

7.6 PAGE VIEWS

This is the number of times your page has been viewed for a specific date range, which can be set at the top of the page. There is also a breakdown of how many times each section was viewed. (Fig. 7.7)

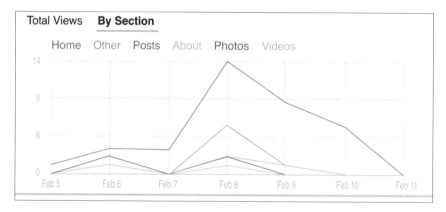

Fig. 7.7

There is a breakdown of the number of people who viewed by page section, age and gender, country, city and by device used. In this section you can also learn how people found your page. Was it on Facebook, Google search or from other social networks?

7.7 ACTIONS

The number of times people took action on your page: like, get directions, clicked on your phone number, clicked on your website link or hit the call to action button on your page. There is also a breakdown for each action by age, gender, country, city and device.

7.8 POSTS

Learn what times of the day and what days your fans use Facebook in the posts section. Use this information to inform what days and time you publish content on your page. (Fig. 7.8)

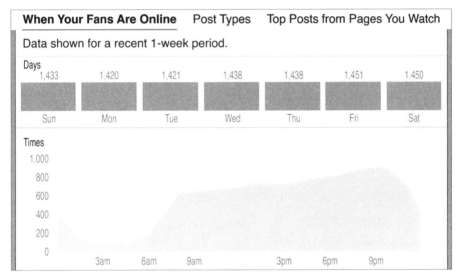

Fig. 7.8

In the tab 'post types' you will get an overview of posts that performed on your page by post type. This will give you an insight into what type of post your fans are most likely to engage with. (Fig. 7.9)

See how engagement levels on your posts compare to posts on pages you are watching in the 'top posts from pages you watch' tab. This gives a summary of the reactions, comments and shares.

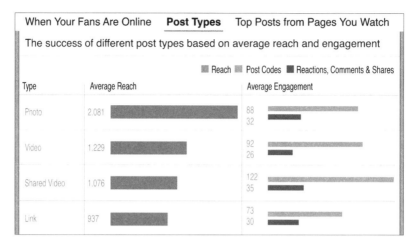

Fig. 7.9

There is also a list of all posts published on your page with a breakdown of:

- Date and time
- A summary of the post – in case you can't remember it
- The type of post – by video, link, image etc.
- Who the post was targeting – global or preferred audience
- Reach – the number of people who saw the post
- Engagement – the number of reactions, comments, shares and clicks
- Promote – see which posts have been boosted and how much was spent. There is also the opportunity to view more data on the promotion.

This is the tab I find most useful in Facebook Insights. It gives an overview of 15 of your most recent posts with the option to view more if required. It's easy to compare posts, to take into consideration the time and the date the posts were published. Have some posts not performed as well as others because of the days of the week or the time of the day? If you're unsure of when to post or how frequently, this is important data for you.

7.9 EVENTS

A summary of how page events have performed in terms of awareness, engagement, tickets, and audience (see section 1.12).

7.10 VIDEOS

Learn how many times videos have been viewed on your page. Facebook considers a video viewed at 3 seconds; a 10 second view is an important marker as at 10 seconds there is brand lift and ad recall.

There is also a summary of the top videos published with a breakdown by date, time, targeting, reach and views. (Fig. 7.10)

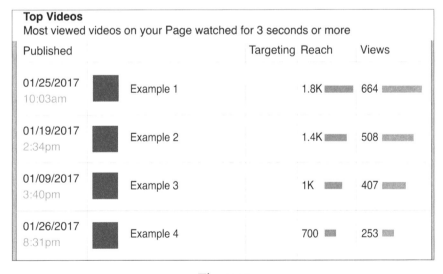

Fig. 7.10

7.11 PEOPLE

This tab is divided into your fans, people reached and people engaged.

- Your fans: Get a breakdown by gender, age, location and language. (Fig. 7.11)

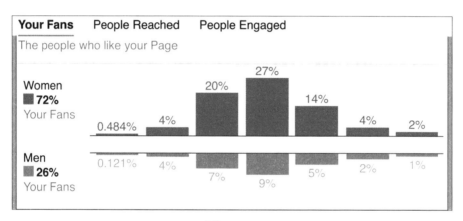

Fig. 7.11

- People reached: A breakdown by gender, age, location and language of the people reached.

- People engaged: A breakdown of the people who liked, commented on, shared your posts or engaged with your page.

- This information is very useful for learning about who you are connecting with and who is most interested. This can be used to create saved audiences for Facebook ads and for other marketing activities outside Facebook.

7.12 LOCAL

Use this tab to learn about the people around your business who are using Facebook. This information is currently only available in the US for local business pages.

7.13 MESSAGES

See a summary of the number of conversations on your page. There is a breakdown of your response rate and average response time.

20% OFF